Praise for *Money Does Grow on Trees, the Family Tree*

"We've worked hard to build a successful business that has made our family financially secure. But when it comes to how to preserve that wealth, how to pass it on effectively to our daughter, and how to teach her about money in an environment much different from the one we grew up in, we didn't have the experience to draw on to know what to do. This book provides a framework for just that. It's about much more than just money. Inside, you'll find the heartfelt letters of a father to his wife and children with practical advice on how to have the important financial discussions needed to create a financial plan—a Life plan—for you and your family."

—CHRIS HEFLEY & KELLY BAKER-HEFLEY

COFOUNDERS, LEANKIT

"This is a great book for people who hate to think about financial planning, which is most of us. With disarming style, the author talks to his wife and children about how the life they want and their finances intertwine. Charming and informative."

—DR. DAVID FURSE

ADJUNCT PROFESSOR, VANDERBILT UNIVERSITY

"In Money Does Grow on Trees, the Family Tree, Trey Smith hits another home run. He makes a difficult subject simple and distills his years of experience in complex finance and investing down to understandable bite-sized chapters that address each stage of a family's life. This will be our 'go-to guide' for family investing and generational estate planning."

—OMAR L. HAMADA, MD, MBA AND TARA N. HAMADA, MD,

PRIMDEVIE TRANSFORMATIONAL HEALTH

THE HAMADÉ GROUP, LLC

"Trey really captures the essence of how families should approach money and lays out a plan that families can follow to be successful. He goes beyond typical financial planning, putting in place a foundation for families where family values come first and drive how and why wealth is achieved by a family that transcends a single generation creating wealth, enabling families to build a set of family values and wealth that can be passed on to multiple generations. I know families will find this book helpful because my wife has been asking me for these answers for years."

—BRAD TICE, PHARMD, MBA, FAPHA

"In Money Does Grow on Trees, the Family Tree, Trey's guidance reminds us that when we add purpose and perspective to our financial plan, we increase the likelihood of happiness and success for our families and those important to us."

—TED AND TAMMY ATWOOD,

COFOUNDERS OF TRAKREF

MONEY DOES GROW ON TREES
THE FAMILY TREE

MONEY DOES GROW ON TREES
THE FAMILY TREE

FINANCIAL WISDOM FOR
INTERGENERATIONAL GROWTH

TREY SMITH
CFP®, CIMA®, CPWA®, ChFC®, CRPC®

Published by Advantage, Charleston, South Carolina.
Member of Advantage Media Group.

ADVANTAGE is a registered trademark and the Advantage colophon is a trademark of Advantage Media Group, Inc.

Printed in the United States of America.

ISBN: 978-1-59932-681-8
LCCN: 2016952577

Cover design by Katie Biondo.

Advantage Media Group is proud to be a part of the Tree Neutral® program. Tree Neutral offsets the number of trees consumed in the production and printing of this book by taking proactive steps such as planting trees in direct proportion to the number of trees used to print books. To learn more about Tree Neutral, please visit **www.treeneutral.com.**

Advantage Media Group is a publisher of business, self-improvement, and professional development books. We help entrepreneurs, business leaders, and professionals share their Stories, Passion, and Knowledge to help others Learn & Grow. Do you have a manuscript or book idea that you would like us to consider for publishing? Please visit **advantagefamily.com** or call **1.866.775.1696.**

TABLE OF CONTENTS

SECTION THREE
FATHERLY ADVICE

A WORD FROM
THE AUTHOR

I have been married nearly two decades to my wife, Dianne, and we have two wonderful daughters, Katelyn and Larissa, who are sixteen and twelve. I started writing this book for them, the women in my life. It began as a series of letters, in case something happened to me—but I realized the basic information and concepts could be useful to many types of families, so I adapted it into a book to share with you.

This is my second book on financial matters. My first, *Tips, Tricks and $ Advice They Don't Teach You in College*, offered common-sense advice to help people starting out in life avoid basic financial mistakes. It was primarily for twentysomethings and my clients who wanted to share some wisdom with their children or grandchildren, especially since twentysomething children seldom admit that their parents actually might know a little bit about life. Sometimes younger generations respond better to advice from anyone other than their parents . . .

This book is different—more personal. When I was writing down my advice to young people, I realized that I also had some things to say to my wife and daughters. These are some of the things I need them to know—at least a start. This is what most spouses and parents want their families to know but often do not know how to tell them—or even if they do, they just never get around to telling them (or don't understand themselves).

In my case, the reality is that Dianne hates talking about money, economics, or really anything that has much to do with what I do for a living. One of the promises I made to her early in our relationship was that I would not discuss my business with her. In an effort to be fair, I should also point out that at the same time I made her promise not to talk to me about any of the details of the surgeries at the animal clinic where she was working. This was of great benefit to me since I am a notorious wimp when it comes to that stuff.

However, her dislike of the topic doesn't mean I shouldn't do the best I can to make sure the family was financially literate. I asked myself if I should simply continue working behind the scenes to plan for our future, especially since as of today, I am healthy and happy (well, I do need to lose some weight) and expect to be around for quite some time—but one can never know for sure what tomorrow will bring. And in reality, is doing it by myself really the best way? Shouldn't Dianne be involved and engaged or at the very least be giving me the direction I need to make sure I am on the right path?

By writing this book, I will know that I am communicating to Dianne, Katelyn, and Larissa what I find to be important on a wide variety of matters (but this book is in no way all-inclusive of what is important). I will also be creating a path for Dianne and me together to share our values and what we want the future of our descendants to not just look like but the values we want it to represent. Growing up in Illinois, we always had a garden, and my father went to great lengths to prepare the soil in order to get the crop he wanted, both for this season and future seasons. Similarly, I think of those values Dianne and I are trying to communicate as the nutrients that will hopefully keep our family tree growing strong long into the future. That is why I am writing these words, and I hope that you, too, will find much of value in these pages. I begin each section by sharing the opening of a letter to my family before I broaden the discussion and invite you in. I end each section with a review of what we have covered and some steps for you to take to begin this process for yourself and those you care about. You may find that these section reviews are a good place to start as you consider your own situation and goals in life.

This book is not designed to be one of the many get-rich-quick books that proliferate the bookstores and instead focuses on essential information in order to help you pass true wealth on to your family. The body of this book will be basic and not highly technical. You will not find deep conversations about market theory or the like. For the most part, the advice in this book will be universal, and some of it will be similar to what I wrote in my previous book because it applies no matter your age.

Being the father of two daughters has made me realize that a major problem with financial services is that the information is geared toward men and doesn't really speak to the concerns of women. Maybe one or both of my daughters will help change that someday! In the meantime, I am pleased to offer a different perspective: a book, written for a family, with a special emphasis on women because the most important people in my life are women. And while

I hope to live a long, long life, I hope all of them are still here when I am gone. After all, this entire project is one way I hope to share my thoughts with them. But the information should apply to your family no matter how it is made up because family is family.

Even though my wife Dianne doesn't happen to care for it, many women are currently in charge of the family finances—either by inclination or by necessity. Even if women do not play the central role in such decisions today, they will likely do so at some point in their lives. Whether single or married, the reality is that women are taking on a larger role in both their financial security and the financial security of their family (often including spouses and parents). Their increased role in the financial outcomes for themselves and their families makes perfect sense when you consider women graduate from college at a higher rate than men, are increasing the number of businesses they start, and outlive us guys. In other words, no matter who is the default finance person today, it pays to prepare—especially because it isn't all about the money.

Recently, at a lakeside cabin during my wife's family reunion, I saw how complex the issues around family and wealth are as they were playing out over the various generations and how they extended beyond just finances into areas such as health, education, and the transfer of family values to the youngest family members. I even jotted down some ideas as I watched everyone chatting and relaxing and the children playing. Each person was at his or her own stage in life, physically, emotionally, and financially. I realized that my guidebook would need to apply to people wherever they found themselves in life. At the same time, I wanted each reader to be able to focus narrowly. Thus, the structure of this book was created.

This topic is especially important to me since, in the history of both sides of my family, I have seen the consequences of failing to plan. This happened even though the two families had completely different stories. They were in widely different businesses; they weren't even geographically similar since one side was from Michigan and the other was from out West. The only real commonalities were that both had attained considerable wealth and that the wealth had failed to make it to my branch of the family tree. They fell into the same trap as so many other families—the old "shirtsleeves to shirtsleeves in three generations" story in which the first generation rises from the fields or factories to create amazing wealth, only to have it squandered by their children and grandchildren. Or as is often the case, the people in the family who take leadership are not the ones who are ideally suited, and flourishing businesses die.

It was partly because of my family history and the stories I had heard that I became interested in financial planning. Through both formal education and witnessing what successful families had been doing for generations, I eventually came across my most important realization and that is that wealth is about far more than money. And if you want financial success to continue, you also need to pass on the very traits that made your family successful.

I am confident that you will find in these pages a foundation for examining and discussing complex issues, concerns, and problems. No matter who you are, no matter what your current role in the family, you will find information that's going to help you and your family stay true to your values as you achieve your goals.

INTRODUCTION

DEAR DIANNE...

Too often it seems that couples never get around to sitting down to talk about the directions they want to take in life. Sometimes those conversations are difficult, and so they never get started; sometimes life just gets in the way. But one of the conversations that is necessary to secure a life together is a financial discussion, reviewing all the steps that a growing family needs to take to position itself for financial success now and into the future.

In most relationships, one spouse or the other takes a strong lead in handling finances while the other takes a back seat. While in the past this might have been a male-dominated role, this is no longer true. In fact, most studies show that more women than men now control the family purse strings.[1]

---

1 Barbara A. Kay, *The $14 Trillion Woman: Your Essential Guide to Engaging the Female Client* (BookSurge Publishing, 2009).

Regardless of gender, some people are more naturally interested in the world of money, while others find it dreadfully boring and want little or nothing to do with financial planning. My own wife, Dianne, would rather not think about monetary matters. Our daughters, Katelyn and Larissa, are still too young, at ages fifteen and twelve, to understand financial planning except at its most rudimentary level appropriate to their age.

And yet, as a financial planner, I know that these are crucial conversations that must take place between couples. Yes, these are conversations that by their nature involve money, but they also broach issues fundamental to the future of a family. Financial planning is often misunderstood as the realm of stockbrokers, market watchers, and investment gurus. But it is much more than that.

Financial planning is, at its heart, life planning, and if either spouse is left out of the equation, how can a couple expect it all to add up? If something were to happen to the primary breadwinner, for example, how would the family go on? How would it move forward with all its hopes and plans and dreams?

Ideally, financial planning involves more than money. It involves the hopes and dreams of a family. Whether the husband is the breadwinner and money manager or the wife holds the purse strings, we all know it takes emotional as well as financial resources to raise children and lead a family into the future.

In my own situation, the question became how could I initiate this critical conversation with Dianne while respecting her clearly stated desire not to be involved in our finances? How could I let her know about the things I wanted her to be thinking about, the things I believe she needed to be aware of? How could we walk together, step by step, along all the pathways of financial planning?

And what about our daughters? If I were out of the picture, would they grow up knowing what they needed to know? I am totally confident that Dianne would nurture them with abundant love to launch them into adulthood. That is her nature. However, because it is also her nature to shy away from financial matters, would our children learn the fundamentals necessary to get a good financial start in life?

I hope that I will be around to share a lot of life and financial lessons with our children, but we all know that tomorrow is not guaranteed to anyone. If we don't lay the groundwork today and communicate our family goals, objectives, and values, tomorrow may simply be too late. Because I have seen this happen to other families, and I knew I did not want it to happen to mine.

FOR MY FAMILY

I am a CERTIFIED FINANCIAL PLANNER™ (CFP®). Day in and day out, I help my clients develop a consistent approach with their families so that everyone knows what is important and what their roles and responsibilities are. I knew that it was high time that my own family took such action, even if Dianne had no interest in discussing financial matters. Certainly if I believed that this was essential for other families, it was essential for my own, too.

I decided that a series of letters, written to both Dianne and our children, would be a good start to imparting the things I wanted them to grasp. I knew that Dianne would read what I wrote about the steps we needed to be taking now, while we both are alive and young (at least in my own mind), with a growing family. And in the letters to our children, I could tell them about issues they would need to consider if Dad were someday not there to guide them through their college years and beyond. I could tell them not only how to handle money but also how to handle life. I could tell them what our family stood for—the values that Dianne and I, together, had embraced, the values that would hopefully turn our family tree into a majestic sequoia that could last a millennia rather than into a Bradford pear. (If you aren't familiar with this variety, they are pretty but short-lived trees that contractors love to plant in every new subdivision, and they break with the first big storm once they mature.)

And so I set out to write those letters. "Dear Dianne," I wrote, and "Dear Katelyn and Larissa"—and out of my pen came page after page of heartfelt advice and practical information. In the pages ahead, at the start of each section, I will share the openings of those letters. As I was writing them, I came to realize that I was also bringing into the picture much of the advice I give to my clients every day.

In every community, there are many families who have not talked about their finances. According to recent studies, approximately 69 percent of parents say that they want to be good financial role models for their children, yet 74 percent say they're reluctant to discuss money matters with their children.[2] They live and dream and die without having these discussions. I recognized that I could help many people beyond just my family and my clients because what I had to say was universal in scope.

A FRAMEWORK FOR DISCUSSION

Time and time again, I have seen that even people who think they have taken care of these matters have seldom crossed all the t's and

---

2 "Parents Bribe Kids for Good Behavior While Behaving Badly Themselves on Money Matters," T. Rowe Price, March 25, 2014, https://www3.troweprice.com/usis/corporate/en/press/t--rowe-price--parents-bribe-kids-for-good-behavior-while-behavi.html?id=39773.

dotted all the i's. They'll have one area of financial planning done but not another, or they won't have explained their reasoning for certain decisions—and that can create animosity, especially among siblings when the expectations of the siblings may not only be different from each other but also from their parents. Another example I have seen involves charitably inclined people whose children had no idea that charity was important to their parents and therefore never carried on their tradition of giving. Simply put, the best chance for a family to succeed over multiple generations is to leave clear directives and expressions of purpose, values, hopes, and goals for future generations to honor.

However, it can be hard to bring up sensitive family issues. You may acknowledge the importance of sharing your thoughts and feelings about money and your family's values, but so many commonplace things can get in the way of doing so. Whether you are attending to some emergency or just trying to relax at the end of a long workday, having a deep discussion with your family over money might never rise to the level of a priority. And it's hard for all of us to talk about the prospect of dying. It comes across as, "If I get run over by a truck tomorrow, this is what I'd like you to know . . ."

For example, in my family, it is much easier for me to talk about the prospects of my death than it would be for my wife and daughters to listen to such talk. Most days they actually like me, but with teenaged daughters, it's only most days. That's why we needed a framework. That's why *every* family needs a framework. You need to be able to keep everyone on track with difficult conversations and bear with it, even when the going gets tough and emotional.

Originally, the most gentle and loving way to approach these matters that I could think of was in the form of letters to my loved ones, which then evolved into this book. This evolution took place because it quickly became clear that this needed to be a conversation between Dianne and I, and the book provided an opportunity to create the activities in the section reviews for you to utilize.

In this book, I could assemble with clarity many of the things that I would like my wife and daughters to understand, now and later. I could express things we needed to do now, while we all are together, and later on, when the time comes that we must part. I could share with Dianne and the girls the principles behind the decisions that were being made on behalf of the family and most importantly have activities we could do together so they could share with me what is most important to them in order for it to be included within the plan. Too often the sharing and inclusion of other's needs is the missing piece.

Although my original motivation was largely to leave my family with some parting advice should I predecease them, I also wanted them to have something we could share in the here and now. Sure, they would need to know what to do if I died, but I also had a lot to say to them right now, while we are here under the same roof, experiencing life and growing together. And through this I learned they had a lot to say to me as well.

With this book, I hope to offer other families some processes and time frames for action. Each section has action items for you and your family to consider. My hope is that these questions and suggestions will help you to create a book of your own to bridge the "financial conversation gap" with your family and share important family values that can be passed from generation to generation.

THE SEASONS OF LIFE

Many people will read this book and be most concerned about not spoiling future generations with a large inheritance—for those people I think Warren Buffet summed up many of their fears when he said, "A very rich person should leave his kids enough to do anything but not enough to do nothing." Others may have no concerns about leaving a large enough inheritance that future generations have no need to be productive but still want to make sure that any inheritance creates fertile ground for future growth. Whether you are starting out today or long since retired, this book can help. This is a book about planning for life, and for that reason it should be valuable to anyone, in any financial circumstances, for any season of life.

The sections of this book show the stages of life based on where my family is today. My first focus is on the here and now, for couples like Dianne and me who are raising a family and building for a future. The next focus is on preparing for the loss of a loved one and how to move on when that happens. And my third focus is on a father's advice to his children, whom he knows will one day take the reins of leadership.

Begin where you will. I started with some words for my wife as we continue to forge a life together. If that's where you are in life, that's where you probably will want to start reading. Those who have lost a spouse may wish to begin with section two. A single person may find that section three is the appropriate place to start. There I have included advice and thoughts on preparing a new generation to carry on the family legacy. Where you start is up to you. My hope is that the advice in this book will help you end up where you want to be: a financially secure family.

IN SEARCH OF THE BIG PICTURE

I want to reiterate, this is not a book designed to teach you how to beat the market. If you have one of those books already, throw it away. To become financially secure, you don't need Wall Street jargon. What you do need are strategies for looking at the big financial picture in your life: What are the consequences of your actions or inaction?

I have always worked with my clients to help them make the most of their resources. With this book, I want to formalize a methodology that can be used to lay out a road map for what readers want to accomplish and the legacy they want to leave. Invariably, things may come up—be they opportunities or misfortunes—for which you did not plan. I will show you how to deal with those contingencies. I have laid the information out on a priority basis. It can be overwhelming to tackle all of your financial objectives at once, so I begin with the most pressing issues and lay out a strategy for dealing with new concerns that arise. Then I will demonstrate a framework for action.

In the final section, I work to prepare the next generation. A lot of people, particularly the wealthy, are wary about revealing the extent of their resources to their children or grandchildren. They fear that young people might not be as productive if they know a big inheritance is waiting for them. But think of it this way: If you were running a $20 million company and decided to step down and retire, would you walk a child into the front office, pat him or her on the back, and say, "Congratulations, it's all yours now"? Or would you ease that child into the business, teaching him or her what you know over time?

It's imperative that the older generation ensures that the younger one understands how to deal with money as well as the goals and expectations of the organization, whether the "organization" is a family or a corporation. Money can be used to do great things, but it is only a tool—and that is why values must be associated with it. Younger people need to understand, as early as possible, the power of money. Once they inherit a sizable sum, it is their experience and maturity that will determine how they handle it. In the same vein, many sudden lottery winners simply squander whatever comes their way. It takes time to develop financial wisdom, and it is every parent's responsibility to teach it. You don't want your children and grandchildren to turn into the equivalent of an unprepared lottery winner with the money you leave them.

> "It takes time to develop financial wisdom, and it is every parent's responsibility to teach it."

A CALL TO EMPOWERMENT

My goal is for the chapters ahead to be empowering for all types of families. Men, women, and children all play important roles in family affairs and must be engaged in the full range of discussions. This book is designed to help the family nurturers be all that they can be and to help couples plan for themselves and for the generations ahead. My hope is that the book will also assist young singles in taking their first steps into the world of wealth management. And I have included information for survivors, who may find themselves looking to the future without the person who, for so long, guided the family's finances.

No matter your situation, this is a book of preparation to help ensure that financial issues do not take you by surprise as you raise a family, buy a house, save for retirement, or grieve at a funeral. The goal of this book is to help you develop your playbook for making successful transitions between all phases of your life.

SECTION ONE
FROM THIS DAY FORWARD

Dear Dianne,

It is that time again. I remember when we first got married, you made me promise not to talk about the stock market at the dinner table anymore because it bored you senseless. Ever since, our agreement has been that I bring it up only when I must.

Well, I have some good news and some bad news. First the bad news: we will need to talk a little bit about the market but only in the broadest terms. Now the good news: let's talk about our future, what we want for ourselves, what we want for ours kids, what we want to give to charity now, and the legacy we want to leave. We will also have to touch on protecting that future if something were to go wrong—but let's not dwell on that this second.

First, the fun stuff!

"Failure to plan is planning to fail."

ANONYMOUS

CHAPTER 1

A COUPLE'S GUIDE

Financial harmony at every stage of life

Many times, despite the best of intentions, a couple's financial planning starts off as a one-sided affair. As I mentioned, that was the case in my family. My wife, Dianne, does not like to discuss anything related to financial planning. She trusts my decisions and has as little involvement as possible.

Nonetheless, I do still need to know what she wants. And because I'm not a mind reader, we do need to discuss these matters at times. Otherwise, my planning for our future is basically guesswork. What I assume she wants might not be what she truly wants. For example, every spouse has bought a birthday present that they thought their partner would love and found out that they didn't know them quite as well as they thought. Financial planning can be like that. Often, a couple's priorities do not fully line up.

However, it is not uncommon for one spouse to handle all the financial affairs, while the other shows little or no interest. For instance, I have seen couples for whom financial planning is simply considered the man's realm. For whatever reason, as they have divided their duties, this is one that they decided the husband would handle. The wife may be perfectly capable but may have other pressing matters to attend to, so this is how they have defined their relationship. Each person has specific areas of responsibility. Sometimes it's an issue of control. I also still see paternalistic attitudes at work, particularly among some older couples (and advisors) who hold fast to traditional roles. Other times it's a cultural trait. Whatever the reason, the spouse who handles the money (regardless of gender) may not feel that the other needs to see the full picture.

A wife (or husband) who seems uninterested in financial planning may be making some incorrect presumptions of her own. Often she may feel that the issues she wants to talk about, such as family matters, are unlikely to be brought to the table, so why bother? Some financial advisors are indeed only willing to talk about investments and performance. They do not deal with broader questions or concerns. If that has been the type of financial planner the couple has been dealing with, it's little wonder that the wife might feel shut out, especially since comprehensive financial planning should involve a whole lot more than just the stock market.

What may come as a surprise to people is that true financial planning is actually harder to do, or occasionally even impossible to do, when it comes to dealing with some men. Many men confuse planning with investment performance and actually reject attempts at broader planning. Whether this is consciously done by male clients or not, the reality is that often attempts by the advisor to bring the spouse to the table are summarily dismissed, and the advisor who is willing and wanting to do true planning is limited to just an investment review. However, performance really has little to do with planning.

An example of this difference, in simple terms, is when you plan for a trip. At the time of writing this book, Dianne and I are planning a family trip to Italy. We have discussed where we are staying, what we want the kids to take away from the trip, what special sites we want to see—the list goes on. We have planned for this trip for months, but we have never really discussed how fast we will travel except in the broadest terms. Yes, we are flying and not taking a boat. One of our tours will be by car instead of walking, so we can see more in a city where we are spending less time than we would like. When planning a trip, speed of travel is the equivalent of performance when doing financial planning. It's easy to look at the speedometer and check my speed or look at a report and check my performance, but neither of those metrics actually tells me if I am having a successful trip—whether it is the trip to Italy or the trip your family takes through the generations. It is true that different approaches work for different couples, but comprehensive communication is a must.

> "It is true that different approaches work for different couples, but comprehensive communication is a must."

Both spouses must be involved to some extent in planning for the family's future. They need to talk openly about where they are heading as a couple and what their life goals are. They need to be on the same page, which is why "mind reading" simply won't work. Two individuals are bound to look at things differently. They will differ in their priorities. They may agree on what they want for their children but disagree on how to attain it. When spouses presume, they often miss the mark. Just as it happens with birthday presents, it certainly happens with the many complicated issues of financial planning.

Once we acknowledge that spouses do not think exactly alike, we can take the next steps. Besides, if they did, wouldn't life be boring? Remember there's more than a little truth to the saying "opposites attract," so each spouse brings different concerns to the financial planning table. And when they do, the results can be quite beneficial, especially when the couple can find a balance of strengths and work together for their mutual benefit. If only one person is working on the plan, it is very difficult to obtain the proper balance.

Women, in my experience, tend to better gauge family life than men do, and they can be more aware of how to best deal with certain issues. They may have a better grasp, for example, on which of the children have greater or lesser degrees of maturity and which may need more nurturing and protecting. A wife often is able to ask just the right questions—ones that her husband might overlook or, in my case when dealing with my teenage daughters, be afraid to ask because he really doesn't want to know the answers.

Although men might not attach as much priority to them, understanding family dynamics are nonetheless essential to the future of the family. Typically, one partner will be more aware of what is going on in their children's lives, and unfortunately for us guys it is seldom us. Certainly it could be the man who has that heightened awareness, but the traditional scenario that I observe, day in and day out among my clients (and my family), is that men prefer to keep to the facts. But invariably those facts are floating on a matrix of emotions and relationships. The facts simply cannot be considered independently when crafting a healthy financial plan that will be fulfilling to all members of the family.

That is why I believe this book will benefit men as well as women. Any one spouse won't know it all: they can't know it all, nor can they do it all. A healthy family will naturally have a division of responsibilities, and a devoted spouse who wants to do right by his or her family will seek the balance of viewpoints necessary to get a proper perspective on the future. Two heads are better than one, and two sets of eyes will see more. Each spouse can help to overcome the other's blind spots.

By now, probably everyone has heard that life expectancy of men is lower than women, and for that reason, a truly caring husband will want his wife to be prepared to go it alone and will want her to be fully involved in the planning. But even if the odds are in her favor, a truly caring wife likewise will want her husband to be prepared to go it alone. In either case, the time will come when one or the other will be gone. At that point, how will the family go on? If the family leader passes on first, what will become of the rest of the family?

It's too easy to just live for today and assume that everything will work out. But, as most of us will acknowledge, life throws curveballs. Troubles and contingencies will come our way. To care is to prepare. If you are the family's financial leader, you will want to make arrangements so that your loved ones will be able to fare well without you. If you are the family's emotional leader, you will want to make sure they have the emotional resources to stay bound as a family unit.

CORNERSTONES OF WEALTH

A family's financial planning involves much more than just investments and money. It is really about creating your life and your legacy, and appropriate investments are just one of the tools you need to achieve your goals. Those tools are not just stocks and bonds; they include education, quality family time, legacy planning, and charitable giving. The overall plan is far broader, and it is not just about dollar signs. It is about living well. It is about family harmony, today and for generations to come. Thus, as you can see, if one of the spouses is uninvolved, much of the big picture can be missed.

Families that succeed for multiple generations have a foundation built upon four cornerstones of wealth. I have never met a successful family that is an exception to this rule. Those cornerstones are: education, human capital, philanthropy, and finance. In many ways, they form the roots of a strong family tree, but even families of great wealth can lose it over the course of a generation or two. With these cornerstones in place, families of lesser means can be amazingly successful at achieving all of their goals and objectives.

Families that invest in these four core areas are the ones that seem to be able to carry on a happy and healthy tradition. They focus on the family unit, spending time together to develop loving bonds and creating the type of individuals they want to lead future generations. In that way, they pay attention to not just their financial capital but also their human capital: their first investment is to prepare themselves by creating the type of person who will be a future leader. Similarly they also place a premium on the value of education, which is a major component of the intellectual cornerstone. In most of those families, education never really stops and isn't limited to just formal education but can also include the arts and hands-on business operations or entrepreneurial activities. The reality is they're always doing something to improve their minds and their situations: learning and sharing that knowledge with younger members of the family. They create a family culture where that is the expectation. This is especially noticeable in some families with a strong entrepreneurial tradition. These families display a phenomenal entrepreneurial spirit, where the elders mentor generation after generation to open new businesses or take current businesses into the future rather than just maintain history.

Virtually all of these families are philanthropically oriented, some in a very large way and others more modestly. Some show their charitable inclinations by donating money, others by doing good works. Again, by their own actions, the older generation paves the way for the younger generation to do likewise, encouraging them to participate and including them in decisions on where and how money, time, and influence will be directed. In that way, they will be able to see the immediate results and help assess whether those choices were wise.

Finance is the fourth cornerstone, and it funds the other three. For that reason it is highly important, but the money is not valuable in and of itself. The true value of finance is its power to enable family members to pursue their goals, devote time to one another, and continue to better themselves as they learn, improve, and reach out to help others. Financial tools create a path to help families reach their goals.

These four cornerstones secure the foundation of a successful family life. As spouses focus on different areas and responsibilities, they can come together to share their strengths for the good of all. This is true financial planning. My experience is that women are often much better at expressing what they are trying to achieve. Many times it is they who see the bigger picture, and that is the mind-set that is essential for successful, true financial planning.

When both spouses understand the breadth of what is involved, they realize it is far more than a chore for one or the other. It is an opportunity to join forces. One spouse may be passionately interested in education and philanthropy, while the other wishes to focus on finance and the development of human capital. Together, they have it all covered. Together, they build a strong foundation. Working alone, one spouse would be unlikely to be effective at setting all the cornerstones in place, resulting in a weak foundation.

ATTITUDES TOWARD MONEY

One thing that can affect a couple's ability to build a strong foundation together is a difference in their attitudes toward money. Most couples are surprised to find how different even their basic attitudes toward money actually are. Our early experiences with money can endure for a lifetime. They can deeply affect people's investment decisions, and those fundamental beliefs may also influence each spouse's outlook about their role in a marriage regarding financial decisions.

Anyone coming into a relationship arrives with baggage of some sort. We all have financial baggage that relates to how we were raised and the relationship we developed toward money, and that can lead to conflict in interpersonal relationships. To make matters worse, some people feel that talking about money is taboo in polite company.

The primary uses of money are as a reward, as a punishment, or as a tool, and those are the most common attitudes that people bring toward handling their finances. As a reward, money can be used to encourage behavior that achieves a certain end. This can be as simple as my practice of occasionally giving my daughter a dollar for scoring a goal in soccer. Or it can take place on a much larger scale, such as a parent gifting shares of a business to a child or providing funds upon graduation from college. You just need to be careful that the lessons are proportionate and appropriate so that everything does not seem measured by monetary gain.

The flipside of using money as a reward is using it as a punishment. Generally that involves an implicit threat and issues of control. We all have heard about parents threatening to remove a recalcitrant child from a will. On a much smaller scale, a parent who threatens to withhold the monthly allowance from a ten-year-old is likewise using money as punishment. And it's really no different from the parent who is doing this with a child who is a twenty-five-year-old and receiving an allowance from a trust that is being threatened.

Knowledgeable people use money as a tool to leverage and develop abilities. Ideally, money is a means to help people achieve their ambitions and goals, such as attaining a degree, donating to worthy causes, or funding a family trip to develop closer bonds. Unfortunately, money can also be a divisive tool. Parents sometimes show favoritism, helping and encouraging one child while discouraging and hindering another, even when their ambitions and abilities are similar.

For that reason, it's time to dispense with the taboos around money. If you do not talk about this powerful force upon family life, you risk grave dangers and can miss wonderful opportunities. You need to understand the source of attitudes toward money and control how you and your family utilize it; otherwise, money looms large in family relationships. Often the taboo itself creates an issue. After all, it is human nature to think about the very things we are told not to—especially when it is a large part of our daily lives. The secrecy itself makes it difficult to attain success and satisfaction, and that alone makes it important to get financial matters out into the open.

Starting these conversations is essential. If there is no conversation, then there can't be any preparation. And without preparation, poor decisions and mistakes will multiply to the point where even the greatest dreams will fade. The mistakes of the elders will not only be repeated in the next generation but can grow larger because there are more resources to use in making them. For example, if no one talked to you about money when you were a child, it is unlikely that you will feel inclined to talk to your own children about money. It can be a hard pattern to break.

It's also hard to break the habit of using money as punishment. For instance, if when you were small, you felt intimidated by the threat that your money could be taken away from you, you're likely to carry that attitude into adulthood, where it might influence your investment decisions. This is also the attitude that you likely will pass on to your own children, resulting in the reality that if money was used to control you, you will tend to use it to control others unless you make an effort to break the pattern.

> **"If there is no conversation, then there can't be any preparation."**

These are ingrained behaviors, for better or for worse. The good news is that you can consciously decide to use money as a tool for good and to model that behavior for the next generation. You are lucky if your own parents took that step, but if they did not, then you have a life-changing opportunity to influence your own family from this point forward.

These good and bad behaviors have a tendency to perpetuate themselves from generation to generation. The only way to stop the bad ones and continue the good ones is by breaking those unhealthy taboos, and the best way to do that is through healthy conversation. We need to identify the themes. If you believe that money holds the power to do great good, you will look for opportunities to use it that way. If you fundamentally fear that you're going to lose money, you likely will be so averse to risk that you will avoid the very things necessary to generate money. If you were taught that past financial success of a family creates a responsibility to do or achieve great things for future generations, you will act on that responsibility, but if you weren't taught that it has any value and you just see it as if you won the gene pool, then you will behave according to that belief system.

Spouses need to talk to each other about the underpinnings of their attitudes about money and attitudes they want their family to have. They need to take a close look inside each other's baggage and talk about what they find there. It might seem easier to ignore these issues, but in the long run, that will lead to stress and unhappiness for them and for future generations.

I knew a gentleman who had come from humble beginnings and whose operative principle was the fear of loss. He married into wealth. His wife had never been concerned about money and had never been taught about the value of saving. He was by nature a saver, and she was a spender. In both families, discussing money had been taboo, so neither spouse was able to talk to the other effectively about their backgrounds and attitudes. They eventually divorced, and I believe that their differences around money and their unwillingness to address the issue was one of the leading causes for their split.

It's a sad story but a powerful lesson. It takes thorough communication and depth of understanding to avoid tensions over money that have their roots in childhood. You will do well to ponder those underpinnings. Your best chance of attaining long-term success lies in overcoming any obstacles that get in the way—including yourself. Then, when you have accomplished your own understanding, imagine the positive model future generations will have to replicate.

When you think about it in simple terms, financial planning involves identifying life goals and how you want them to play out. In doing so, you rally the resources necessary to meet those ends. You assess whether you have sufficient resources, and you make the necessary adjustments. Along the way, you cover the what-ifs because things inevitably won't go perfectly. You won't know exactly what you might face, but you can still plan for the contingencies. But there is one thing that definition leaves out—the fact that you have to discuss it. After all, rallying the resources includes bringing in your team and family throughout the process.

CHAPTER 2
WHAT'S IT ALL ABOUT?

Money only matters if you have a goal

We all travel the interstate at seventy miles per hour (and if you are me occasionally a bit more). But if we went through a school zone at that speed, we not only risk a hefty speeding ticket but also lives. Obviously what is appropriate on the interstate is not a good idea in a school zone. Similarly, if you go the school zone speed limit of fifteen miles per hour on the interstate, that won't work out well for you either.

When it comes to money matters, a similar principle is at work. Whether you should put the pedal to the metal with your investments depends upon your current situation. You need to consider where you are, what's ahead, and what risks you face.

Unfortunately, many financial advisors are primarily concerned about the performance of investments, but there needs to be a destination and purpose to drive those investments. Much like that trip to Italy I mentioned previously, a successful outcome depends on whether you are going at the right speed and in the right direction.

In other words, what are the current conditions, and what are you trying to achieve? What is your destination, and what is the best way to get there? To go fast just for the sake of being fast or to outpace your friends is not only pointless but also dangerous. On the flipside, once you are out of the school zone, if you are still crawling at fifteen miles an hour and everyone around you is honking to pass, you clearly need to make some adjustments.

Many times, people use rules of thumb based upon age to make decisions, but just like driving, your investments do not necessarily depend upon your age. I have some younger clients with a lower risk tolerance who are facing particular financial concerns and therefore spending more of their time in the "school zone." I also have clients in their seventies and eighties who have been highly successful and can afford to take on some additional market risk and are comfortable with risk. They can afford to go cruising out on the highway. Remember the proper speed depends upon individual and family situations and comfort levels and will likely change throughout time based upon experience and needs. Often within a family you will see different risk profiles, with some members being highly aggressive and others conservative. These differences are important considerations for planning and multigenerational planning in particular because the effect of different compounding rates over long periods of time is significant.

Regardless of the speed, you need to be headed in the right direction. For example, some people will tie up assets that they might need to use relatively soon, forcing them to sell at an inopportune time or even borrow to cover the need. Others have too much liquidity and would be better off investing some of their assets for the longer term; they could be missing out on a better return and on tax benefits.

Unless you know your destination, how can you possibly determine the best route to take and how far and how fast you need to go? For example, can you walk there, or do you need a jet? Could you take a sports car, or will you need a jeep?

You must map out what you want to achieve. If you're driving from New York to California, it's not enough just to know that you should generally head west (although that's obviously better than heading east). If you simply aim your car westward, you might get to California someday, but it will take you a lot longer than if you do a little planning.

By pulling out a map (does anyone actually use maps anymore?) or using your GPS (much more likely), you can plot your course far more efficiently. You will still need to cross deserts and mountain ranges, but you will be able to anticipate when they are coming and know the best way to get through them safely and expediently. You will know whether you can zip across the open stretch ahead or if you will be edging around mountain curves at fifteen miles an hour. You will be aware of when you are about to cross the desert and need to fill up with gas or when you can stretch it for a few more miles.

The same holds true for your financial and investment "trip." Once you have a destination, you will want to make sure you are heading in the right direction, but you will also want to take the time to plot your course so that you reach your goals in a timely manner while enjoying life. Occasional, planned detours can be what make life worth living. After all, if you are passing close to the Grand

Canyon, aren't you going to want to plan to stop? The key is to know that you are not giving up your priorities for the detour. Similarly, you can adjust and correct your portfolio as necessary so that you are investing appropriately and according to current conditions. Sometimes you will be pressing the gas pedal, and other times you will be tapping the brake in order to take one of those unexpected detours life has a tendency to give us.

However, even a map may not be able to tell you whether a given route is under construction or where there are bumps in the road. You may be surprised by detours and traffic jams. A GPS may do a better job of alerting you, but nonetheless you can be sure that somewhere along the way, something will hold you up—whether it's an unforeseen blizzard, the world's largest ball of twine, or a flat tire. As you plan your trip, you can figure in the extra time that those inevitable (and fun) delays will require and make certain your spare tire is inflated because sometimes a little insurance goes a long way. That's one of the many benefits of thorough financial planning.

A FOCUS ON GOALS, NOT INDEXES

As you can see, the design of an investment portfolio must be tailored to the needs and desires of the individual. Your success will depend on how you are progressing toward your own unique goals. Often, people think that they are supposed to match or beat some arbitrary market index. It's not that those indexes are unimportant. As an investment professional, I watch them closely. But if you have a specific goal that requires you to achieve a certain return, then those benchmarks shouldn't really matter to you. Just as if the speed limit on the interstate is seventy, that really doesn't matter if you are currently in a fifteen-mile-per-hour school zone or vice versa. Instead, you need to create a plan that fits you and your family's needs and is set to the speed that is appropriate to you.

Here is another way to think about it: no one lives in a perfectly average house. My house is designed to suit how the members of my family interact and relate, and it is appropriate for our family goals. Your house no doubt is different than mine and fits your family goals. In the same way, your financial portfolio no doubt is different than mine. Like your house, your portfolio depends on where you are in life and how things are playing out for you. A larger house is not necessarily a better one if now is the time for you to downsize. Conversely, you may be getting ready for children and/or grandchildren and need something larger—you might even want a second home at the beach to encourage family to visit. For most people, trying to beat some arbitrary benchmark does much more harm than good.

> **"For most people, trying to beat some arbitrary benchmark does much more harm than good."**

They take on more risk than they should and do so without a sense of purpose other than beating that index. That makes no more sense than if someone told you that the average speed for all drivers is forty-five miles per hour, and you took that as your goal. Would you be happy if you were beating that average and doing fifty miles per hour on the interstate? I know I wouldn't. Or how about doing fifty miles per hour in a school zone? Again, that's probably not a good choice. Your family situation may require a greater or lesser return than the index, and over your life, that will change too. Sometimes we are in the financial equivalent of the interstate, and its full steam ahead; sometimes we are in the financial equivalent of a school zone, and risks are everywhere and can appear unexpectedly.

It is important to be clear about your situation so that you can invest intelligently, not haphazardly or based on an arbitrary benchmark. You do not want to go too fast or too slow, and the proper pace is determined by the conditions on the road and in your life, not some arbitrary index or magazine article. And importantly, no matter which spouse is in the driver's seat, they both need to stay alert as they set out together to navigate toward the destination of their dreams and to create a legacy that can carry into the future generations that will make up their family tree.

THREE TYPES OF COUPLES

In my experience, when I start to help couples or individuals begin planning and pick the road that is right for them, I have found that generally there are three types I deal with. One type is the *conscious planners*. They establish their goals and set out to get there as quickly as possible. They work consistently toward the successful life that they have envisioned.

I call the second type *unconscious planners*. They know the general direction they want to go in and attend to the basics but not much more. Their planning is mostly guesswork—they save but are not sure if it is the right amount. They do estate planning, but it is so generic that it may or may not work for their family. The financial-planning work they have done is better than nothing, and they deserve credit for that, but they are more or less living moment by moment and either sacrificing too much today and not living the life they could be, or they are being too optimistic and are likely to fall short of their long-term goals.

The third type of couple never plans for anything. They take life as it comes, hoping that they will get lucky. They try not to get caught up in worries, and planning seems like a bother to them. These couples seldom end up where they would like to be, if they even know where that is. They always seem to be encountering problems, and financial stress leads to family and marital stress. Perhaps they ran a successful business, but they never figured out how to transition the business or the assets from the sale of the business in such a way to achieve their goals or even to create a legacy for their family. They might feel that they are on a good path because life seems okay today, but their failure to plan will catch up with them eventually—and if not with them, it will catch up with their children and grandchildren.

The great news is that no matter which type of planner you have been in the past, you have an opportunity to become a conscious planner. And the act of becoming a conscious planner not only will affect your life but can create a strong trunk to help future generations of your family tree to thrive. After all, it is the trunk that holds the weight of the tree and carries the nutrients up to those future generations. The key is simply to broaden how you think about planning (as we have been discussing so far in the book) and to get started.

GETTING STARTED

Regardless of which type of planner you started out as, financial planning means different things to different people and even changes at different times in life. Often it is relatively simple; sometimes, the needs are far more complex. Even though there isn't a one-size-fits-all plan, you still can follow some common practices that have been proven to be nearly universal.

Any financial plan should start with a conversation involving some basics. You need to take a close look at the lifestyle that you want to have and the type of legacy that you want to leave. You will be talking about more than money; the values upon which you base these decisions must be central to the conversation. You need to identify all the goals that you wish to attain throughout your life, not simply the financial ones.

In other words, you need to clearly identify where you are starting, where you're going, how you will get there, and what you will do when you arrive. As I discussed before, you should not judge yourself on how you do against some arbitrary index; rather, consider whether you are achieving what you have identified to be important to you. That is the primary benchmark to identify—not some arbitrary number but what is actually meaningful to you. Through this book, my aim is to help you become conscious planners and to live by design and pursue purpose. This is a process that takes time. In my practice, many couples start working with me only in regard to investments, and I slowly try to nudge them in the direction of broader planning. I may even give them a book to get them started—a somewhat less-than-subtle hint—but it can help get them on the right path, as I hope this book will help you get on the path of conscious planners.

IDENTIFYING DREAMS

Whether you are young and starting out or older and retired, the questions about your dreams and goals are the ones that get to the heart of financial planning. Write them down as a tangible part of your financial plan. Who and what are important to you? Whom do you wish to help? Where do you wish to travel, and what do you hope to learn? What makes you feel happy and fulfilled? As a couple, what are the qualities that each of you bring to the relationship so that, together, you can do more than either of you might do alone?

In order for you to feel successful three years from now, what will need to have happened? How about five years from now? Twenty years? No client ever has told me, after five years of working together, that the most important thing that has happened to them over the past five years was how well they had done against the Dow or the S&P. Instead, their priorities have always revolved around what was happening to their family, their business, or charities they love. The conversation focused on whether they were in a better position to achieve their goals and objectives. The goal may be as simple as the ability to stop working at their job or to sell their business. They may want to go back to school or pay for a child or grandchild to go to school. They may dream about a trip around the world. Perhaps they want to donate a building to the local university, fund a chair, or affect society in some other meaningful way.

Many of those goals will require money or the freedom of time that money allows. By working together with a qualified financial advisor to achieve your aims—whether for one year, five years, or twenty years—you will feel a different type of success, either because you have reached your goals or you clearly see how and when you can get there. It's not necessarily a measure of what is in your investment account but of what you can accomplish. For many, the investment account just gives them the freedom to move beyond a concern for basic needs, allowing them to focus on and achieve their most heartfelt goals.

I have known extraordinarily wealthy people who have not felt personally successful. Certainly they knew that they had created (or possibly inherited) financial success or were great business leaders, but they still felt something was missing. More than once I have had a person who is deemed *successful* by society say, "Is this all there is?" And often these are the very people who are most at risk of going down dangerous paths to reach fulfillment and end up self-destructing, often taking their families down with them. That's because they never did the things that would make them *feel* happy and successful. I also have seen folks whose wealth was more modest but who had accomplished everything that was important to them. I bet you can guess who is happier and who has a happier family.

PLANNING FOR LIFE

Different goals require different time frames. Once you have your goals, one of the first steps will be to establish their time frames. However, it is important not to sacrifice the longer-term goals for the sake of accomplishing the shorter-term goals (or vice versa). Life is a balance, and goals' priorities should be based on their importance to your family and not just time frame or ease of accomplishment.

For example, inexperienced financial planners sometimes over-emphasize short-term sacrifice for long-term gain. In a perfect world that makes sense, but none of us can be sure whether we or our loved ones will be here tomorrow, let alone twenty years from now. What you should be looking for is *balance*. You need to pursue the successes that you can have today while gathering the resources for the successes you want to have tomorrow.

Often a person will identify their family as the most important thing to them but continue working for endless hours every week even when they no longer need to do so. They have already done a good job financially, but they have not checked where they currently stand or even stopped to consider what is most important to them and their family. A good financial planner can help people identify when they have enough resources to stop. We can even try to nudge them in a different direction, but we have to be careful. After all, it is your dream, and it is based on what you enjoy, and sometimes a person's work is also their passion. And although it may be second to their family, they would rather work four more hours than play golf for those four hours.

For example, I love what I do; I generally feel like I help people. I spend much of my free time continuing to improve my skills. Frankly, it probably makes me a little boring, but as I look forward to mentoring new generations of planners, I don't think I ever want to stop. But I also know that family is extremely important to me,

> **"If I haven't made it clear yet, a comprehensive financial plan is *more* than an investment plan and *more* than an estate plan."**

and finding a balance is part of my family's financial plan. Planning doesn't always mean retirement—each of us has our own road to take. My point is that I chose my road rather than blindly driving down it just because that is where life was taking me. And let's make sure that we understand when it is time to take a break, whether for a quick pit stop or for the rest of our lives.

If I haven't made it clear yet, a comprehensive financial plan is *more* than an investment plan and *more* than an estate plan. It's not just about money, and it's not just about who will get what once you pass away. It's not just a retirement plan. Instead, it is a life plan. It should be designed to provide you little victories along the way that will bring you a sense of achievement and to set your family up for future successes long after you are gone.

NO PLACE FOR SURPRISES

How to begin? You need a baseline. As with any trip, you need to know your current coordinates before you can map anything out. And the truth is that many people simply do not have any idea of where they are. A lot of folks are pleasantly surprised once all the numbers are added up. Others, once those numbers are added and the liabilities are subtracted, feel quite the contrary.

Either way, you *need* to know. Are your dreams realistic, or do you potentially have the financial room for larger dreams? Often a family's most fulfilling dreams are not the most expensive but the most time-consuming. You can't know until you clearly define them.

As I work with my wife Dianne, we both understand that I have a better grasp of what we are capable of accomplishing financially and what sacrifices may be needed if we decide to undertake more. It amounts to figuring out where life stands for us today and determining the adjustments we will need to make going forward. If we decide to upgrade our lifestyle or go after a particular goal, then we need to be aware of the give-and-take that will be required. No matter how wealthy you are, resources are limited. We feel blessed to be able to travel frequently, but we also place a high value on keeping our daughters in private school. As with most families, there are trade-offs. Even if only one spouse is handling the money, both must be involved in setting goals and dreaming together.

If the first phase is figuring out where you are today, the second phase is figuring out what your ideal would be. You divide your priorities into things that you need to have happen, things that you would like to have happen, and your wishes for what would happen in a perfect world. People of means who plan and live modestly are likely to attain many of their wishes. Others might realize relatively few wishes if they aren't planned for, no matter what resources they start out with.

That is why it's important to prioritize. First, list the goals that are most important—the things that you can't imagine living without accomplishing. Then list the pursuits that you would certainly find worthwhile but which would not leave you terribly broken up if they didn't happen. Finally, list the wishes you hope to accomplish but only after you can accomplish the rest of the list first.

OPPORTUNITIES LOST

When I began in this industry, back in the late 1990s, one of the first people with whom I worked was an anesthesiologist. He was about sixty-five years old and had been married for a decade. He and his wife had had a child together, a nine-year-old boy.

They had never done any planning. The first time we sat down together, I realized that neither of them had any idea of what they owned nor what they owed. He had always just assumed he was wealthy because he had a significant income, so when they married she assumed the same. The reality was that the family had lived a happy and enjoyable life but had spent almost every penny they made.

At our first meeting, we started talking about their goals and objectives. The savings totaled only about three months' worth of his salary, yet they were hoping he could retire when he was seventy and maintain their current lifestyle. It immediately became obvious that goal was not a possibility, and deep down, he knew it when he came to visit me. To accomplish this, the family would need to save all of his earnings over the next five years to cover him, his wife, and their child for the rest of their lives. Without a dramatic lifestyle change, he would never be able to retire. With a much younger wife and a young child, he had to come clean with his wife and they needed to adjust their goals. This caused them to really look at what their priorities were for the first time in their marriage. Priorities changed, and they started planning for schooling costs instead of retirement and how to provide for the family if something were to happen to him. Fortunately he had the option of continuing to work and was not facing a situation where he would be forced to retire upon turning sixty-five.

The good doctor somehow had never come to the realization that just because you make good money, you can't get from point A to point B if you do not save any of that money. He was exceptionally good at what he did, and he was incredibly smart. But he had never contemplated the personal money side of things. This was a family that had to seriously adjust their expectations and priorities. But with that knowledge came the power to make those modifications, and the family was better off because of it.

Fortunately, among the clients with whom I deal, it is more common that their expectations are adjusted in the other direction—that is, they have more than they realize and could be enjoying a less frugal lifestyle. This is often the case for the first-generation wealth builders.

In some cases, these are people who never had much and always felt that they needed to save. They have long been in the habit of putting money away, a little here and a little there. They have sort of scattered it and never really sat down to take stock of all these pools of resources. In and of themselves, none of these funds were huge. But if you have ten accounts with $1 million in each and you get them working together in a consolidated effort, that can move the needle.

Often, with clients who were business owners, every free penny went into the business. They kept on working and earning and living the same basic life. They never looked up and recognized that they could liquidate that business and reap its true value. Similarly, a lot of the executives with whom I work have been of modest means until the last five or ten years of their careers, when the options, stock, and other lucrative benefits finally begin to blossom in meaningful ways. They hadn't taken the time to think it all through and realize that their net worth was drastically different than it was a decade earlier.

I find it interesting that so many of them seem to notice exactly how much they pay in taxes but do not realize how much income they have earned. "I can't believe I'm spending $400,000 in income taxes," they say, "I don't even make $400,000." They do not seem to grasp that they actually made $1.3 million that year.

Widows and widowers misjudge their financial position more acutely than most couples, even if they have significant resources—especially when the deceased spouse managed the money alone. This is probably because the survivor does not have a frame of reference, was not part of the planning process, and never realized that his or her wealth had increased; they just remember the lean early years. You would be amazed how often one spouse keeps the other completely in the dark about their wealth. All of a sudden, the survivor has not only lost the love of his or her life but also the person who was holding the keys to the castle, the person whom he or she had trusted implicitly for decades to take care of his or her financial future. Even though survivors may now be wealthy, they unfortunately don't have a frame of reference to know whether they will be financially all right.

Perspective is essential if you are to forge a productive future, and that is why couples need to make sure they are of a like mind and have a common destination. Down the line, when a loved one passes, such planning reassures the survivor that the money is there and the goals and the dreams are still in place. So many people just do not know what their current situation means relative to their needs, and that lack of knowledge adds stress to an already painful situation.

It's sad when dreams fade, particularly when it is from unnecessary fear. Fear keeps people from making charitable donations or even taking that family trip to Italy. Instead, lacking knowledge, they replace dreams with stress and confusion. Sometimes making the stress disappear is just a matter of knowing that you are still on the path you planned, the next step is already decided, and all you have to do is take it.

CHAPTER 3

A TEAM ON YOUR SIDE

Guidance you can trust at every step

When I first started my practice, I had a client—we'll call him Richard—who kept bragging to me about how well he was doing at picking stocks for his personal account. When he came to the office, he would tell me stories about how he picked some little stock that tripled in a week.

After a while, I began to wonder why such an equities genius had me managing a single penny for him. Then one day his certified public accountant (CPA) called to ask if there were any gains that could be harvested (for tax purposes) from the accounts that I managed for Richard. His question confused me. Normally an accountant would be looking for losses that could be harvested to offset gains, not vice versa.

I explained to the CPA that the account that I managed for Richard was up and that he had some relatively large gains but, from the way Richard had been bragging, I presumed his personal account had done even better. I asked the obvious question: "Why do you need me to harvest gains with all the great picks Richard has made over the last year?"

The CPA laughed and confided in me that Richard had lost over $50,000 in the market that year. The CPA was hoping to take advantage of those losses by offsetting any gains in the accounts managed by me.

Astonished, I questioned the accountant about the success stories that Richard had told me. He laughed again. Richard did pick winners frequently, he said. In fact, because he traded daily, he averaged about one a week. Unfortunately, his personal account had not had a positive year in two decades. Richard's losers always outnumbered his winners, the CPA said. Richard just never bragged about those losers.

Eventually I learned that several of Richard's associates, impressed by his self-proclaimed prowess, followed his investment advice unquestioningly. When I met them, they would talk about him in awe and remark on how they could never match Richard's performances. In fact, they had felt lucky to break even. What they never realized was that Richard was probably doing worse than they were.

Unfortunately, this is a common phenomenon. Investors trumpet their winners and fail to mention their losers, persuading their friends and colleagues to follow their lead. They're like the old fisherman who says, "I caught one *this* big" and then stretches his arms out. The reality is that unless a person is in your exact position, you want the exact results that person is getting, *and* they tell you the *whole* story, their advice is useless. It may even be dangerous.

GETTING THE RIGHT ADVICE

This doesn't mean you should never talk to anyone about your finances or give any recommendations yourself. I believe that you should get recommendations from friends, family members, and coworkers but *not* about specific investments.

Instead, ask if they have great relationships with their advisors. If they do, inquire about what they like the most and what they like the least about how their advisors work. If they are extremely happy, ask if they will give referrals. Do the same in return.

It's beyond me why people tend to ask one another for product advice instead of asking for a referral to a competent advisor. It would be a little like asking a friend who had been cured of a specific disease to recommend a drug instead of asking which doctor remedied the problem. I'm sure you would agree that the doctor, not the friend, should be the one to diagnose your specific condition and prescribe the best treatment for you.

It never fails to give me a chuckle when clients tell me that a coworker has given them a hot tip. It seems that there is a person in everyone's life who gives the impression (whether on purpose or not) that they are a financial genius.

Regrettably, even if a friend has done well for himself or herself, it has little bearing on whether or not that friend's advice will do well for you. Just as in sports, being a good player does not make you a good coach or even a good player at the next level. In high school, I was judged to be a good athlete and made all-conference in football. Does that mean I should have gone pro? At 5'9" and 160 pounds?

Today, the average high school kicker is probably fifty pounds heavier than I was when I played.

It seems that if a person appears to do well financially, everyone assumes they are competent to dispense financial advice. This simply is not the case, just as my successes in high school football did not entitle me to become a professional coach.

To be a great coach, it takes knowledge and training about the entire game, not just personal experience or skills in that area. Similarly, if a friend is truly proficient in one area of investing, you are still at risk when following his or her advice because his or her range of knowledge will probably be limited.

A true financial planner weighs the pros and cons of all financial products and understands how to apply them to a client's unique situation. This is far different from the friend who may have generated significant wealth in real estate, for example, and

> "To be a great coach, it takes knowledge and training about the entire game, not just personal experience or skills in that area."

suggests a similar strategy for you—even if the market has changed or you do not have the time, skills, or resources to run a real estate conglomerate.

An analogy I often use when I try and explain this phenomenon is the restaurant analogy. At one time or another, we have all been told about a great restaurant. You know, the one you simply "must try," only to find out it is crawling with kids. The food may be great, but if your goal is a romantic evening, the ambiance leaves a lot to be desired.

The problem is not the restaurant but the circumstances. The family that recommended the restaurant may have found it ideal because they were comfortable and couldn't hear their kids screaming over everyone else's. It would have been a great recommendation for another family. But if your goal was to have a romantic evening, it was probably not a great one for you.

Those of us with families have also had the reverse happen. After a soccer match, we head with the kids in tow into what we were told was a great casual restaurant, only to find out that the wine list is two pages long and they do not have a children's menu. Again, both of these restaurants may be fabulous, and the referrer may have excellent taste, but neither of those facts makes the recommendation suitable for your situation at that specific time.

In reality, almost every financial product is perfectly designed for someone. The question is whether you are that someone. And if you are, is this the right time for you to invest?

Even if you have someone who can see past their own personal situation, there remains one more catch: everyone naturally discounts what they have been unsuccessful at or what they do not understand. This means that the more complicated the concept, the more likely someone else is going to say you should never do it. This is especially true for men. The cliché about a man never asking for directions all too often holds true for financial matters as well. And worst of all, instead of asking the question and admitting a lack of knowledge, they just say no.

Unfortunately, that confusion can extend to professional advisors. For example, take permanent insurance. For those in the right tax bracket, it can be a phenomenal solution. But there are many incompetent people selling it, so it has earned a bad repu-tation. Complexity, mixed with highly competitive commissions, has created more than one problem over the years. However, if you review the estate plans of the wealthiest Americans, you will almost always find permanent insurance in one of its various forms. The key is in working with competent agents and not rookies or fly-by-night companies. Normally it is not the product that's the problem; the problem is how the product is used.

Remember, the more complex a product, the greater the likelihood that someone will say it's a bad idea. That is true whether it's a personal preference, a lack of knowledge, or a product that really doesn't fit—the problem is knowing which of these is the case.

We all live in different houses, like different cars, enjoy different foods, have different goals, and have different experiences in general. Just because something did or didn't work for someone else doesn't mean it will have the same effect on you.

THE POWER OF DELEGATION

Many of my clients were, at one time or another, do-it-yourselfers. There are times I even recommend for you to go it alone. After all, ultimately it's you, not your advisor, who lives with the results. Even if you do hand over all your financial decisions to someone else, you still have made the most important decision: to trust that individual with your finances. In that way, no one ever stops being a DIYer.

However, most people have blind spots when it comes to financial planning. The blind spots could be with insurance (some folks believe they are going to live forever), equities, or any of the other myriad financial concepts and structures. The simple risk is that you do not know what you do not know, and even if you realize that you have a gap, you may not consider the time commitment required to learn the skills necessary to fill it. You might become good at one part of the financial puzzle but leave yourself open to unnecessary risk or lower returns. For example, alternative products may be necessary to balance portfolios or lower risk, but few individual investors can access them without a professional's help.

However, if you are still determined to be a DIYer, my advice is to start with something small. This way, if you make a mistake, you can still recover. For example, if you enjoy investing, consider maintaining an account you personally manage. After identifying your goals and objectives and ensuring that those are covered, you can set up what I refer to as a "Vegas account." This is a sum of money, the loss of which would not stop you from achieving your goals—and if you did well, you could move those goals forward to be even greater. A Vegas account also allows you the opportunity to express your investment savvy without having to devote your full time to managing the overall family financial plan.

Because you have completed a plan and set aside a specific amount that will not affect it, you can rest assured that your needs and wants in life will be fulfilled regardless of the performance of your Vegas account. Even I have divided my own money into a serious account, to take care of long-term goals, and what I nicknamed my hobby (or Vegas) account, where I take much greater risks. If you have the resources to do that, just realize that this is basically money that you have designated for play because *retirement is not a hobby*.

The reality is that I have never met anyone whose image of an ideal retirement is sitting and staring at a computer screen all day, watching the stock market. That is really just a change of careers. However, if such a person exists, I would have to wonder just how that person's spouse feels about it. Dianne has commented more than once that she expects us to do things together, and I doubt she was talking about trading stocks.

For most, just as failure to plan will ultimately lead to anxiety, so will micromanaging your finances on a daily basis. For that reason, many people who want to enjoy their retirement decide that it is best to delegate that responsibility.

Often, people will begin investing as a hobby while they are working or running their business because their job or business is providing for them and their family. In those situations, it is great when things go well, and as long as those people have planned and know they are saving properly, it is not a disaster if they make a mistake. When they get to the point of retirement, that dynamic changes because it then ceases to be a hobby and becomes a new full-time job. And the cost of failure at that new job can be very high.

It isn't an issue of intelligence. In fact, it is the most intelligent who realize that they have and regularly use the power of delegation. A great example of this is surgeons. We all know they do not operate on themselves, and they generally won't do even minor operations on their loved ones.

When I used that example with a client who is a doctor, he said, "I would not want to take that risk with any of my loved ones," and then he paused and followed it with, "Except maybe my mother-in-law," giving his wife a wicked smile. His smile was short-lived as his wife responded: "I'm not sure my mother counts as one of your *loved ones!*" He may have ended up sleeping on the couch that night.

Wise surgeons don't operate on loved ones, even when they are experts in the field. They also don't operate alone; instead they operate with an entire team, with each member bringing their own skill sets. The reality is that managing your own money in retirement (or any of your important financial goals) is not minor surgery. You are tackling a serious procedure. You need an impartial perspective from a steady hand and a team for support.

ORGANIZING YOUR TEAM

Just like those surgeons, you need an expert team as well. You may be okay starting off on your own, but once you reach a certain level, it is time for a professional team.

It generally works best if you have one person who coordinates the team. Ideally you will have an annual or biannual meeting with your entire advisory board, including your CPA, lawyer, planner, and occasionally your insurance person. Normally, the planner who ties it all together will also be the investment person, but if that person only does investments, you probably need someone else on the team to coordinate.

Through it all, your objective is to achieve your family's goals and to gain expertise. One of the biggest concerns for many individuals is whether or not they're giving up control when hiring an advisor. In the best of situations, the clients are the ones who make the big decisions. What they're looking for are folks who can help them to make the best decisions, coach them through that process, and then help implement the plan. Just as in athletics, executives and speakers often benefit from professional coaching. After all, it only makes sense that you get the best results when working with people who have developed expertise in their field.

After all, having control does not mean having competence. Someone may be calling the shots, but many people still need advisors to fill them in on the best information needed to make good choices. There is no shame in not knowing how to do everything. The best CEOs know they need to delegate responsibility. The president has a cabinet. Almost every great leader had great council—and listened to them. The best leaders determine the destination and bring together the people with the know-how to accomplish the task.

Most of my clients have been working with specialists for decades. They have a banker for standard bank issues, brokers for investments, accountants for their annual taxes, and lawyers to help with their businesses and estate documents. More and more frequently I even see trustees for trust management and concierge medical services.

Depending on your needs of the moment, some people may play multiple roles. Someone will serve as a quarterback for the team and may also play the role of coach. Normally that is the person with whom you have most of your contact. Generally, the person who will serve you well as your total financial advisor will be the one who is willing to sit down with you, look at the comprehensive picture, make suggestions on a variety of different financial manners, and bring together all the members of the team in a coordinated fashion. That is an essential role because the investment advisor needs to know what the estate planner is doing, and they need to work with the tax expert and the others on the team. Mistakes can cost millions of dollars, often with money going to the IRS instead of to the family.

IT'S A FAMILY AFFAIR

However, the most important members of the team are the family. It starts with you and your spouse, and when appropriate, includes other members of the family. That doesn't mean both partners have to be at every meeting, but it is essential that both spouses meet the team, even if only one primarily handles financial affairs, especially since at some point, he or she may be depending on the team. If you were the surviving spouse, would you want to be in a position of walking into a room full of strangers who are supposed to help you with financial planning after the funeral? This is a time of grief, and the introduction of the team should not come at such a stressful time.

Often, a surviving spouse will switch advisors simply because he or she does not know any of the financial team members. Since they were never introduced, no relationship has developed over the years so there is no trust. He or she may not even realize the advisory team has been working hard with the spouse to create a masterful plan. And even if they do, often the surviving spouse ends up feeling that it was not designed with his or her dreams in mind. Would you trust a team you had never dealt with or that had never asked you what your goals were? In other words, the best-laid plan with the best team is for naught if both partners don't agree or, worse yet, if one partner doesn't even know the plan exists and that there is a team to help implement it.

This doesn't just apply to spouses but also to the children when they are old enough. Children should be involved in the financial plan or at the very least meet the team and be aware a plan exists. Often this isn't the case, because wealthy families are concerned about causing damage to their children, and so they keep financial discussions discreet. I have observed, however, that it often does more damage when the children are not involved. Not preparing them for an inheritance is not protection; at best, it delays a potential problem, and sometimes it actually creates a new problem.

As your children become adults with families of their own, they often are aware that they will be inheriting assets. What they don't know is how it will affect their own financial plans. For example, do they need to save to pay for their children's college education? Often, children are embarrassed to ask whether their parents are planning to help the grandchildren with educational costs or other expenses. Sometimes this means that they are saving unnecessarily, but other times they assume they will get help, so they don't save at all, creating a need gap when they are wrong. Uninformed children feel in the dark, and this often leads to stress in the family.

Another scenario that happens frequently deals with clients who are either the first generation of true wealth (i.e. worth considerably more than their parents) or who have become wealthy in their own right before a potential inheritance is even a consideration. In either scenario, they do not need their parents' money, and if asked, they might prefer that it skip their generation and go straight to the grandchildren. If both generations of the family are open and asking the right questions, this can be arranged. This first generation of wealth may even be worried about the roles and responsibilities they will be taking on as their parents get older, especially if they're the first children in the family to have financial success, if they do not know their parents' plans, or if their parents have enough wealth in their own right to take care of themselves as they age. A great example of this is arrangements for long-term care. Not knowing if arrangements have been made or if the duties will fall on you can weigh heavily. Yet most of the time, no one wants to ask. After all, who wants to even think about their parents being in need of help? But through planning, this can be addressed as just one more item to discuss.

Parents can make their children's lives easier by letting them in on the planning. They can reassure them that certain arrangements have been made and tell them what plans are in place in case one of the parents becomes debilitated. Certainly, children need to be notified if they have been given health-care directives or durable power of attorney. Too often, the first time children find out about that responsibility is when a parent becomes incapacitated, and at that point, they still haven't been told what the parent's wishes are. If you are the child who is in the dark, it is important that you try to open up this conversation with your parents. If you aren't comfortable doing it directly, one way is to involve your parents with your team. Financial professionals are often used to dealing with multigenerational families, and although we can't share information between generations (unless specifically directed to by the individual whose information it is), we often can encourage the generations to have better communication among themselves by initiating a dialogue and discussing how these concerns affect families in broad terms.

> "Very often the money conversation and the values conversation need to go hand in hand."

Much of the communication will be oriented toward money, but often a part of the conversation takes place around expectations for carrying on the family mantle and the family name. People tend to focus on the financial side, which obviously is important, but there are also more emotional concerns that families need to address.

Very often the money conversation and the values conversation need to go hand in hand. Families always want the children to be responsible, and there definitely is a risk if you give a child too much too soon, especially without the proper training. But that risk doesn't necessarily get better with age, although people often assume it does. If you drop $20 million on an unprepared sixty-five-year-old, they are no more or less likely, in my experience, to waste it than a twenty-five-year-old.

To avoid that, the heirs need to be educated on how to handle money responsibly. They need to understand that money does not equal happiness. There are a lot of very wealthy, unhappy people, and there are a lot of happy people who have yet to attain wealth. Fulfillment trumps financial wealth, but of course a combination of the two is best. A caring family should help the successive generations prepare for wealth while also allowing and encouraging them to find their own path first. At that point, the additional success that wealth can provide will not be a burden but another tool for future success. If they have been mentored to be their own person and have their own successes before the wealth appears, it will make them more confident when the wealth does come. And they in turn can provide the mentoring and training the next generation needs to avoid the stupid mistakes that so many people make when they receive wealth.

When wealthy families have trouble with a child, often it is because the child is not comfortable in his or her own skin and does not know how to deal with being in the shadow of the family's wealth. If these children have no success or confidence in their own right, they often feel guilty or even resentful of the wealth they are set to receive, when it should be a blessing. Children who have developed some success independently will likely feel more grounded and will become better stewards of those dollars. They won't feel that they have something to prove.

One of my favorite sayings in regards to this is, "Fulfillment leads to success, and success leads to wealth." Often, if the wealth comes before success, the heirs will squander it because they do not appreciate it and are too insecure to handle it.

Preparing your heirs for inheriting wealth is a lifelong endeavor. The earlier you start, the better, but that does not mean you need to share too much information too soon. It does mean that you occasionally have to say no when asked for resources, even if you can afford to provide them. In that way your heirs can learn that resources are not unlimited and can come to appreciate that they have to make choices about money. To become productive members of society, they need to know the value of a dollar. Otherwise, the adage of "shirtsleeves to shirtsleeves in three generations" is likely to prove true.

People ask why the shirtsleeve adage is so often true, and the simple answer is that it comes down to math and a lack of long-term planning. Here's a simplified example (see illustration 1) of what so often happens. Picture a couple retiring in 1955. They had the equivalent of $20 million in today's dollars, and each generation only spends growth leaving the original value but not allowing it to increase with inflation. For most people, the first shock is the effect of inflation. In 1955 it only took about $2.2 million to have roughly the same spending power as $20 million in 2015 (in other words, a dollar bought a lot more back then). This is important because although $20 million may seem like a relatively large amount today, sixty years from now when your grandchildren inherit the family fortune, it will not be nearly as significant. This is especially true if we assume similar inflation for the next sixty years as we have seen for the last sixty years.

Okay, now that you see the impact of inflation, what about the basic growth of the family tree? Let's assume a typical family with two children split the assets equally between the two children upon their passing thirty years later. With each child inheriting $1.1 million and decreased financial pressure for raising children (remember they are utilizing the growth to assist their lifestyle, and in the 1980s a million dollars was still significant), one heir has four children and the other heir has two children. Then, at the second generation's passing thirty years later, each grandchild eventually would inherit between $275,000 and $550,000, depending on how many siblings they had. For those of you who are from the same TV generation I am, this example might remind you of the Fabergé shampoo commercial from the 1980s, where the TV screen fills up with an ever-increasing number of shrinking faces with the model saying in the background "and they tell two friends, and they tell two friends" until the screen is full. Surprisingly, you can find the commercial on YouTube if you are really bored or curious. Now back to my example. The wealth creators who retired in 1955 probably would have still thought an inheritance of over $250,000 sounded good but only because they never thought to adjust it for sixty years of inflation.

ILLUSTRATION 1

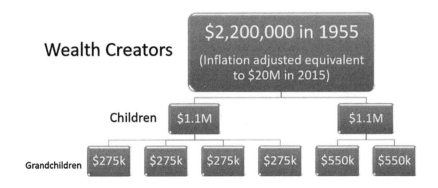

It takes multigenerational knowledge and discipline to keep that from happening. The money needs to be managed in a way that keeps ahead of inflation and battles the other forces that can dissipate wealth. The first step is to recognize that these forces are at work, and that is just another reason you need to involve the family to the degree they are ready and capable and to begin to prepare them if they aren't ready or capable at the moment.

WHAT TO LOOK FOR
IN AN ADVISOR

Whenever you are choosing an advisor, you should look for people who have demonstrated that they are serious about what they are doing, have reached out into the professional community, and have continued their own education.

Knowing what the letters after an advisor's name mean is important in making sure that you find someone qualified. Those titles will give you an indication of the value that the advisor will bring to you. Some designations are quite difficult to acquire and represent many hours of study and work; others are relatively easy to get. Online resources can help you research those designations to help you decide whether a particular advisor possesses the qualifications to suit your purposes.

Above all, you need to be able to connect with your advisor and communicate with ease and openness. He or she should have the people skills to work effectively with you, your family, and your professional team. You will be sharing a lot—and not just numbers on a page.

I have seen raw emotions surface during the course of discussions with clients. There can be touchy issues, particularly those involving transitional planning and inheritances. Sometimes a couple has never before aired their concerns and frustrations regarding their goals and objectives. They may face hard decisions involving children, step-children, and their children's spouses. Most wealthy families often incorporate trusts, for example, arranging for the funds to stay in the bloodline in the event of a divorce or death. Those are not pleasant issues to contemplate, but they must not be pushed aside.

Fortunately, the talks usually do go smoothly. Spouses are often pleasantly surprised to find that they are on the same page or just that their voice is being heard. However, there still may be a lot of work to do, and some tough conversations will be necessary on the way to a successful and fulfilling financial plan. This is why it is so important to find an advisor you are comfortable with and whom you can trust.

CHAPTER 4

THE FAMILY GUIDEBOOK

A written legacy of values and beliefs

L egacies involve so much more than money. You are leaving behind your values and your principles as well—the story of who you were and what you believed. However, your family also needs some specific information and directions to help it move forward. A family guidebook is a valuable means by which you can communicate matters of both heart and mind.

The family guidebook helps to ensure that your name and the things that are most important to you will be remembered for more than just a generation or two, and it is an heirloom of sorts that can be passed from branch to branch on the family tree. For this reason, in the review at the end of this section, I have included a template of steps and questions that will help you in this process. I also offer suggestions on how that family guidebook can be expanded into a multigenerational family book as each generation adds its own chapter. In that way, your children and grandchildren will more clearly understand your character and will not have to guess at what your wishes were, and they can add their own perspectives and wishes for their own heirs.

Some people will work with their team to help them in the creation of their family guidebook while still doing some of the more personal parts alone. The point is that you decide what to include and how to build your family's guidebook in order to reach your desired results. Regardless of the details, what is most important is that you pass on a portrait of who you were and what your family should stand for. No one size fits everyone, and you can create any variety of book you like utilizing all of the resources available to you.

THE INFORMATIONAL ASPECTS

The family guidebook can have multiple parts, one of which will just be informational and not be designed to be passed on from generation to generation. A simple example is that you will need to include a list of your computer log-ins and passwords. For obvious reasons, this portion of the guidebook will need to be kept in a very secure place, like a safety deposit box, but there can be a note saying how to access it. This simple act can help the family avoid the common hassle of getting locked out of crucial accounts that need immediate attention in case of emergency or death. The letter also can direct your heirs to the people whom you trusted to be your advisors. It can tell them where you keep your documents and provide a summary of their contents.

In that way, the guidebook is a list of directions. It says, in effect, "Here is where you can find information on all the accounts, here are the passwords, and here is a list of my investments." Dianne does not know, or want to know, about all the investments I have undertaken on our behalf. But one day she certainly might need to know, and the letter gives me an opportunity to conveniently list them for her.

Many people think having assets properly titled for ownership is enough, but it isn't. You have to make sure your loved ones know that these assets exist and where and how to access information about them. Fifteen million orphaned 401(k) accounts, representing more than $1 trillion in investment, littered the financial landscape in 2010.[3] That includes IRAs, bank accounts, and other investment accounts, and if you didn't catch that ,it was a trillion, with a just for the 401(k)s in 2010.

> "Dianne does not know, or want to know, about all the investments I have undertaken on our behalf. But one day she certainly might *need* to know, and the letter gives me an opportunity to conveniently list them for her."

Can you imagine how the balances of all the different accounts have grown since then?

I have some personal experience both from family stories of how CDs were opened in Canada by my great-grandfather just to be safe (but never were found) and a personal investment I opened in college. When I was eighteen, I invested a small amount of money

---

3 Paula Gladych, "Orphaned 401(k) accounts stacking up," Benefitspro, May 9, 2013, http://www.benefitspro.com/2013/05/09/orphaned-401k-accounts-stacking-up.

directly with a mutual fund family. But since it was a small amount, I eventually forgot I had opened it. After several years with no contact and returned envelopes because of address changes, the fund family decided that it was orphaned and forgotten. Then one day I got a cryptic letter from a company telling me that I had left some money, and they were willing to split it with me because they knew where it was and I didn't. Fortunately for me they jogged my memory and I was able to call the fund family directly to claim the funds. But because they were funds that predated Dianne, she would have had no idea of what these shysters were talking about. This is just one function of the family letter: to provide those lists, locations, and directions. Think of it as handing over your maps and keys to those you love.

However, that type of information is only part of what the family guidebook is all about. And it might just be the easiest part because it primarily engages your head rather than your heart.

A RECORD OF YOUR VALUES

The second part of the family letter is much more personal. This can be part of the same document, or you may wish to draft a separate document to be shared while you are alive. This part of the guidebook involves how you wish to be remembered. You will tell your family things you want them to know and understand about you as the generations move forward. These were your hopes and desires. This is what you believe. This is what you value. This is the story of *you.* If you think of the family tree symbolism we have discussed, this is the trunk of the tree. It is the one thing that keeps each branch connected with each other.

Too often there is a disconnect between generations. A family creates significant wealth, and by the third generation, it seems that no one has any clear idea of how the wealth was even created. They remember the name of the company, perhaps, and have a fairly good idea about what it did and who it served, but they do not know the story of how it was created or about the hard work of the early days. They know little or nothing about the ingredients of that success. They can only guess at what their grandparents envisioned for them.

If you imagine your own descendants being similarly puzzled about your intentions and dreams, then consider putting it all in writing. The family guidebook is how you can preserve those values and memories for generations to come. Tell them about the faith and charity and hard work that were important to you. You want those qualities to be dear to your children's children as well, and this part of the family guidebook will be your record for posterity. At least they will know that these were your dreams and expectations for them. This was the legacy you hoped to bestow upon them.

Writing the family guidebook is not just about expressing warm and fuzzy feelings. The truth of the matter is that without a foundational understanding of the family values, money seldom endures. It evaporates in the ensuing generations as it falls into the hands of people without purpose. This is a model that has been observed in cultures around the world. For example, in Asia, it is known as "rice paddy to rice paddy in three generations." Unless the first generation to rise from a life of labor is able to maintain the momentum and lessons learned, the family is likely to lose its way and eventually return to a state of far more modest means.

That requires more than just a letter saying, "I loved you with all my heart." Those are sweet words, of course, and hopefully you have had plenty of opportunity to say them while you are alive.

Instead, the letter is your opportunity to say such things as: "We were charitable, and we want you to continue that spirit," or "We grew our wealth because we wanted you to start out with more than we did. We envision every generation of our family doing the same for the next one. We expect you to continue growing the wealth and not simply spending it." In effect, you are codifying how you wish your family to behave. You are giving them rules for living, based not simply on a whim or some investment philosophy but on what is important to you and what made you a family that achieved success.

THE RIGHT APPROACH

You may be wondering what the proper approach is to creating such a guidebook. Do you assemble your entire family and talk it through? Or is this a matter for husband and wife to work out? Should you consult with your business associates and tap into their wisdom? Do you write this out by hand on a notebook in front of the fireplace, or do you engage professional help in drafting the letter?

The answer is that it can be done in any or in all of those ways. Normally, however, it starts with the generation who generated the wealth.

The best way to start is to sit quietly and jot down some initial notes on what matters most to you as you envision your family going forward. What will the young people need to know? What do you wish you had known at their age? Perhaps you were born with entrepreneurial powers but probably not. You likely attained success through trial and error. The progress probably came with its share of pain, initially. What mistakes did you make that you hope will not be repeated? What mistakes do you think it is important for them to learn on their own? Maybe you will tell them the reality that it is okay to make mistakes. You would be surprised at how many of the most successful people in the world had huge failures in the beginning and how many of their children are afraid to make a single mistake. Write about what you have learned through experience in life and in business, as well as what you believe in your heart to be true.

Once you have gained a degree of clarity on what you want for the next generations, you can open the conversation to others in your family, your network of friends that you respect, or possibly even other families who have had multigenerational success. Gather their perspectives and insights. What have been the governing principles by which their family as a whole has found success?

Each family will be different. Some families are highly charitable, and they want to make sure that the family continues the legacy of giving back to the community or to a certain cause. In other families, education might be a priority. The mark of success, they believe, is when each child embraces the life of a scholar. Others believe success comes by perpetuating the entrepreneurial spirit; each child should be looking for new and profitable pursuits and taking the appropriate risks to grow the wealth. Other families dearly value a tradition of public service or political office. And some families emphasize their faith.

Think of it this way: if you could see your family members fifty or one hundred years from now, what would they be doing that would make you feel proud? What attitudes would they be expressing to their own offspring? When you start thinking along those lines, the ideas will begin to flow. You will be able to express the story of how you grew your wealth and the sacrifices that were involved.

Because the guidebook also will include many specifics on how to move forward in business and in life, it is important that the family guidebook be made in conjunction with thorough financial planning. You'll want to consider many elements such as estate planning and business succession. You can delineate, for example, your intentions for control of the family business and your reasoning for that decision. However, those choices should be made in the course of professional planning so that you will know the specifics. You want your legal documents and your family guidebook to be coordinated for consistency.

Those specifics aside, the guidebook, in large part, will amount to a mission statement for the family. It will sum up strategies for success. Many children simply do not know that their parents or grandparents were charitably inclined or how proud they were to be the first in the family to go to college (or maybe even just graduate from high school). They are unaware that their elders donated money to certain causes or institutions. By sharing that history, you will be opening their eyes.

EXPLAINING YOUR RATIONALE

Writing the guidebook also creates an opportunity to talk about why you are setting things up in certain ways. If you have established trusts, you can tell your loved ones why you have done that. If some provision is not to their liking, they at least will see your reasoning and understand that they need not take it personally.

For example, Diane and I have set up a trust for ourselves, with our children one day having access to the assets. However, if they marry, their spouses will not have that access. We wish the money to stay in our bloodline. At the time of writing this book, our daughters are twelve and fifteen. We do not consider it our responsibility to take care of whomever they someday marry. Our job is to provide for our children and potentially for our grandchildren. They and their spouses presumably will have the character to make their own provisions on behalf of each other because it's the right thing to do. Knowing that we thought that through long ago, the girls will know we meant no slight against whomever they chose to marry and that they need to take some responsibility for those they bring into the family.

The guidebook is also an opportunity to explain your reasoning if you have divided the estate into something other than equal shares for each child. They may not like it, but they should be able to understand it. Often what a parent does out of love is not the way the child would have it. Your children are not all the same—they have different strengths, abilities, and inclinations—and you may well decide to adjust the inheritances accordingly. You may decide to divide the estate equitably in ways that do not all involve the immediate assets. The saying you often hear in reference to doctors is applicable: "Do no harm." Of course, the hope is that you will also be doing some good.

AN ACT OF LOVE

The family guidebook does not necessarily have to be written as a book. Successful families sometimes do this in the form of a letter, but sometimes they pass on these traditions and stories and values orally. Some families produce a recording or a video for the future generations. There's no right or wrong way to do this. The book, letter, or recording can be as specific as you wish. It can include detailed information on trusts and foundations, or it can be far more general, dealing mostly with themes and principles. You can even break it up so that people only have access to certain parts at certain ages or certain events. For example, you could have a part that is available to the family at any time, an additional part for when they are about to get married or reach a certain age, and a final section that may not be revealed until your passing. Each family can find the fit that is right for them.

Remember this is an act of love. Its goal is to help your family avoid the haze of confusion that so often comes after the funeral. "What did Dad and Mom really want?" "What are we expected to do now?" That confusion can lead to dissension. Your

"**You are communicating what you believe to be the fundamentals that tie your family together, and as the generations pass, they will be able to measure themselves against those ideals.**"

clear directive will prevent that. Your family will not be guessing, and at times when there is so much emotional pain due to loss they will deeply appreciate your clarity and this reminder of who you are.

You are communicating what you believe to be the fundamentals that tie your family together, and as the generations pass, they will be able to measure themselves against those ideals. That will be part of their inheritance—indeed, the most important part. They will be getting the story along with the money. Somehow, when the story accompanies the cash, there is less squabbling. The younger generation is more likely to feel the desire to maintain and grow the family legacy. It goes from a sense of entitlement to a sense of tradition and obligation to future generations.

SECTION ONE REVIEW

Congratulations! You have completed the first section, and you should be better prepared to begin the groundwork of your financial planning.

First, here are some highlights of these first four chapters:

- If you are in a committed relationship, both of you need to participate in the planning.
- Effective planning involves deeper issues than simply determining when you will retire. That is particularly true if you have a family and want to leave a meaningful legacy.
- Know when to get help. Almost everyone who achieves great things has a coach. In today's world, it is not a sign of weakness; it is a sign of professionalism.
- Build a team that works for you. Even if you are trying to manage your financial planning on your own, you should have at least one reliable professional as a sounding board for your decisions.
- Begin building your family guidebook because the legacy you want to leave is about much more than money.

How to Get Started

As couples work together, they will need to ask each other a variety of questions. Here are some helpful hints to make the most of the process:

- As you get started, relax. After all, you will be discussing your dreams.
- Break the discussion up into manageable pieces. You may feel that you can discuss your whole list of questions in a

single sitting, or you may wish to take it a single question at a time. There is no right way or wrong way—just get started, and keep up the progress.

- If you find yourself stuck or unable to agree on a particular point, do not let it stop you. Move on to another topic. Some discussions will take far longer than others. It was years before Dianne and I agreed on an estate plan.

- First things first. Different couples have different priorities, so there is no right answer. However, consider what has been keeping you up at night. It normally would be best to tackle that first. Decide which dreams you must not sacrifice. What objectives might you postpone?

- Do not wait to start planning until you have everything decided. If you do, it might be a long time before you take any action, and by then your original goals might have changed. Remember the old saying about how to eat an elephant, one bite at a time. Normally when I start working with people, we begin with matters that will have the most meaningful and immediate consequences: the most important goals or perhaps some of the easiest tasks. In many cases a family will develop new goals over the years as they accomplish (or at least are on the path to accomplishing) their old goals. They often want to do more as they become more aware of what is possible.

- If all else fails, sometimes a glass of wine will help.

Here are some great questions with which to begin. For each, an effective follow-up question is, "Why?" Also make sure you keep a copy of each answer because you may utilize them again in the family guidebook.

GENERAL

- What keeps you up at night?
- What makes you feel successful?
- What is the one thing for which you want to be remembered?
- Why is money important to you?
- What are you most passionate about?
- How do you define risk?
- Where do you see yourself in five years? Ten years? Twenty years? Thirty years?
- If money were not an issue, what would you be doing with your time?
- If you could only accomplish one thing in this process, what would it be? (This will probably be the first thing you need to accomplish as part of the planning process.)

FAMILY

- For whom are you financially responsible?
- If something happens to you, what preparations have you made for those people?
- For whom might you have other potential responsibilities? For example, will you be a caregiver to a parent?
- Do you want to be involved in the financial lives of your children and grandchildren?

- What type of legacy do you want to leave them?
- How do you want them to remember you?
- What values do you want to pass on?
- What do your spouse and children find important? Do you want to help them achieve those goals?

CHARITY

- What are you passionate about?
- Do you want to be recognized for your giving or to remain anonymous? Or would you like someone else to be recognized?
- Do you want to share that passion with your family?
- Do you want to create a legacy and expectation of giving for your family?
- How important to you are the tax advantages you could get from some forms of charitable giving?

HUMAN CAPITAL

- How are you investing in yourself and your family?
  - Education
  - Health
- Do you want to incorporate travel in your human capital plan? Would that travel include other generations of your family?
- Do you want to create a legacy of investing in the human capital of future generations of your family?

FINANCE

- Have you selected your team and coach?
- Do they have the credentials and expertise you are looking for? Do you know what those credentials mean? Do you understand the different types of advisors?
- How have the members of your team been continuing their financial education?
- How have you been continuing your own financial education? (Note: This does not need to be formal, and your team could provide it.)
- Are you preparing your family for the financial legacy that you plan to leave to them? (Note: This is important whether you are leaving great wealth or relatively little.)
- To maintain your ideal lifestyle, how much income do you need?
- If you own a business, do you have a plan for its succession?

NEXT STEPS

- Pull together the necessary information. If you do not have everything, do not let that stop you. Most people gather it over time.
- Here are some fundamentals to include:
  - anything that comes on a statement (If the information is online, make sure you include the user ID and password.)
  - any real estate holdings, including documentation of ownership and any liabilities
  - private equity holdings, including ownership and liabilities
  - the value of any assets and liabilities that do not have statements

- insurance documents
- your last tax return and previous years if they vary significantly
- the amount of your annual savings, if any
- any potential inheritance because that could significantly affect your plans

FINAL STEPS

- Decide who will be on your team. At least one person on your team should be a CFP®. Other designations indicate particular specialties. (I have several, most of which reflect my specialty in working with high-net-worth individuals.) Be sure that your advisor has experience with clientele whose needs and concerns are similar to yours, and find someone you can trust. Working with a team does not eliminate the risk of fraud, but it does decrease the risk—there are more people to potentially catch a bad player.
- If you are a DIYer, find at least one person to be a sounding board. Then begin reading additional planning books and online information on the various elements of financial planning. Do not skip topics that you do not like. You must avoid blind spots.
- Create a family guidebook (see the following steps).

Creating a Family Guidebook

In section one of this book, we discussed the value of a family guidebook, but I did not include many details as to what to include. I also alluded to the fact that it should be much more than a set of directions while not telling you what or how to actually put it together. The good news is that I am going to fill in some of those blanks, but I am still avoiding creating a strict style you must follow because I believe each family can create their own unique structure to house it, and the section by itself could fill an entire book.

One way to think about the family guidebook is similar to a travel guidebook, but rather than learning about locations, you are passing on information through future generations of your family tree. And just like a travel guide needs updates, each successive generation will add their own chapters and photographs to keep the family guidebook up with the times.

Your family guidebook will consist of at least two primary sections. The first section revolves around financial information and directions. In simplest terms, these are the directions for dealing with the financial issues of your estate when you die. For this reason, each generation of the family will need to completely recreate this section for themselves because a hundred years from now the information you place in this first section may be interesting from a historical perspective but it won't carry the same weight as the items in the second section, which will be much more meaningful on a personal level.

These are not exhaustive lists but merely a good place to start. Use your imagination of what you would have wanted to know if you were the person that was going to have to read this after your passing.

Having said that, at the very least it should include copies of the following (or at a minimum where to find them):

- team names and information (one person can fill multiple roles)
  - lawyer
  - CPA
  - banker
  - investment advisor

- ▫ insurance advisor
- safety deposit box location(s)
- copies of estate-planning documents (keep originals in safe locations)
  - ▫ wills
  - ▫ trusts
  - ▫ power of attorney—although not a true estate document since you have to be alive for them to be used
- financial information including firms, account numbers, and contact person for the following:
  - ▫ insurance policies
  - ▫ investment account numbers
  - ▫ bank statements (including liabilities)
- financial information for private transactions (at a minimum includes names of either the entity or individual, contact information, and supporting documentation)
  - ▫ private equity
  - ▫ partnerships
  - ▫ private debt
  - ▫ deeds (homes, cars, other real estate)
  - ▫ valuable items (list provided for P&C agent is a good place to start)
    - o jewelry
    - o art
    - o collectibles
  - ▫ tax return (can help track accounts or income items such as royalties that may have been otherwise missed)

The second section is much more personal, and I recommend it be done in a printed format although you could also use a video format, but if you elect a video format remember technology changes over time and the formats utilized today may not be accessible in the future.

This is my recommended format and order, but as I mentioned, this section is much more personal so feel free to add or subtract, combine (for example a photo with a story immediately following), or rearrange sections to suit your needs.

- Create and document your family mission statement (family philosophy).
  - Since creating a mission statement is a process in its own right, I recommend you read or listen to "How to Develop Your Family Mission Statement" by Stephen Covey. The audio version is just a little over an hour.
- What do you want your family name to be known for (here are some examples)?
  - entrepreneurship
  - education
  - philanthropy
  - art
  - service to your country
- What family traditions do you hope endure for generations?
  - Why?
  - If it is already a family tradition, a heartwarming story is a nice touch here.
- What values and concepts of importance should be included (see questions from the beginning of the section review)?
- Utilize the questions you discussed at the very beginning of the section review, and discuss which of your answers

are timeless and that you hope future generations will incorporate into their plan.

▫ Why?

• Include at least four family photographs. Make certain each person in a photograph is named, or over time the names will be lost.

▫ the earliest known photo of the person or of the couple together

▫ a photo of the couple when they entered a committed relationship (if still together)

▫ a photo of the family as each baby was born

▫ a photo of the entire family that includes as many generations as possible

• Include family stories.

▫ Where did you meet?

▫ What was your most challenging experience? How did you overcome it?

▫ What was your greatest failure? What did you learn from it?

▫ What was your greatest success? What did you learn from it?

▫ What are you most proud of? Why?

▫ What mistake did you make that you hope future generations won't repeat?

SECTION TWO
AT DEATH WE DO PART

Dear Dianne,

I am sorry. I didn't want to leave you and the girls, and deep down I think I always hoped I could live forever to be there with you and to continue to watch the girls grow. I guess if you are reading this, it didn't quite work out that way. I know that if I were with you now, there is one thing you would want me to say. I know it's a poor substitute to say it in writing, but here it is.

Everything is going to be all right!

Okay, now let's get started. First, take a deep breath. Don't do anything before you are ready. We have already done a lot of preparation in case this were to happen, so let that process start to run its course. There will be some things we missed or changed, and that's okay. We'll take this one step at a time. Don't rush.

I know you and trust you, and you have everything you need to do great. Have confidence in yourself, and follow the plan we worked on together . . .

"Great questioning leads to great awakening. Little questioning leads to little awakening. No questioning leads to no awakening."

ZEN SAYING

CHAPTER 5
A TIME TO GRIEVE

Getting affairs in order

S tories on both sides of my family are one of the reasons I became interested in financial planning, as well as why I believe planning involves more than just the money. Back in the 1930s, my family operated the original motorized moving vans in Detroit, Michigan. My great-grandfather was a strong man (at least that is what I hear) and passed away at a relatively young age. As was normal for that generation, he had been the patriarch of the family, controlling the entire business.

Unfortunately, the family was not prepared for his early death. No successors had been trained and mentored to run the operations. It wasn't even clear who was supposed to take control, but back in those days one thing was known—women were not considered businesspeople. Fortunately this myth is quickly disappearing, and wives and daughters are often the chosen successor for today's family business, however, at the time the family sent my great-grandmother away to Cuba for a month to try and relax. In the meantime, the leadership fell into the hands of someone who was not properly prepared to take over operations. The consequences were disastrous for the company. Trusts were broken, and the business eventually failed, which resulted in the wealth completely evaporating within a generation.

A business succession plan could have saved the family company, and in the same way, it is essential to have a succession plan for your family if you want it to survive and hopefully even thrive. Just as when the owner of a business passes away, someone of competence and sound training must be prepared and ready to take over, whether they are just managing their inheritance or end up with broader responsibilities; like a family business, often other family members or future generations may depend upon an inheritance. For this reason, the leadership must not default to whoever seems available and inter-ested. Often, the person with nothing better to do has neither the experience nor the fortitude and ends up being the worst choice.

It happens in countless families. A business owner who has run a company successfully for many years refuses to step aside or even to let anyone else become part of it. Under their control the business has generated significant wealth and income for the family, and the business is a phenomenal success. But their persona is so closely tied to the business they cannot imagine stepping down or see who else in the family might run the business half as well.

And then one day, being mortal, they are gone. And the family left unprepared is unable to carry on because nobody has been trained to fill those shoes. In such situations, the surviving family members may feel regretful or even angry. And often the business only survives the original proprietor's passing by a couple of years or at most a generation.

Whether we are talking about a family business or an inheritance from a successful executive, the results are often the same if the inheritors are unprepared or if the assumed choice is the only person available and willing to take on the role, rather than the best person for the job.

This is a somewhat less common scenario in younger families, but in older generations, it was usually the case that the husband handled the finances and was the executive or ran the family business while the wife handled other family matters, and then it was the oldest son who took responsibilities for financial matters when something happened to Dad and the oldest daughter who took care of the parents' health and welfare when they started to fade. Today, roles have changed, and it is often the wife who has enjoyed amazing success and takes care of the finances, while the husband handles the rest. Either way, when a family loses a member, they will need to fill a major gap—and whether they can do that successfully will depend on how much advance planning has been done. As anyone who knows me will attest, even though Dianne doesn't handle the family finances, her loss would be devastating to me, and an equal amount of planning needs to take place in case of her loss as is the case if something were to happen to me.

DIFFICULT CONVERSATIONS

It can be hard to plan for your own family, and that, in large part, is why I am writing this book. Even as a CFP®, I need feedback from my wife. Some of the conversations are fun, as we talk about our dreams, but others can be a bit depressing.

Nonetheless, the conversations you do not want to have are normally the most meaningful ones. One of my jobs is to help families anticipate how they will deal with the loss of loved ones. Those can be productive conversations, but people can get emotional when dealing with these issues. I understand how it feels. It isn't fun for me when Dianne and I start talking about our estate plan and contemplate a time when we won't be together. That's never a fun conversation for couples (at least, I hope it

> **"Nonetheless, the conversations you do not want to have are normally the most meaningful ones."**

isn't). But making sure that we are prepared for that time is part of our responsibility to each other. As with most couples, Dianne handles certain aspects of our family life, I deal with others, and each of us needs to know what to do in case the other is gone.

A great personal example of this happened one weekend as I worked on this book. Dianne and Katelyn were away at a soccer tournament, and I was at home editing my book and waiting on Larissa to return from a sleepover. It doesn't sound like a big deal—I actually had twenty-four hours to myself, and my only obligation was our two mutts, Shelby our pound puppy and Leo the Morkie. Yes, to my surprise, a Morkie is a real dog. Most of the time I still think Leo more closely resembles a long-haired guinea pig than a dog, but since he is the only other surviving male in the house, I have to give him at least a little respect.

Then I saw the list. You see, one of our dogs, Shelby, is a bit old, okay really old, which means she is half blind, half deaf, arthritic, and evidently has allergies. (I honestly think Dianne just made that last one up to annoy me.) I have to admit, I do spoil her and feed her table scraps regularly, so the vet also tells Dianne the dog is fat and needs to go on a diet. To my surprise and chagrin, this dog is on a more complicated drug regimen than most ninety-year-olds, and I have to feed her green beans at every meal to boot so she will lose weight. I can't even get my daughters to eat green beans.

What I thought of as twenty-four hours of freedom now involved me being a home health-care provider for Shelby. That's a long story to say that without Dianne and her line-by-line instructions who knows what havoc I could do to Shelby's health and what unforeseen emergency it would create. Obviously Shelby's normal regime would fall through the cracks, but what other unforeseen things would have, as well? Dianne prepared me with a list of the important items for when she was away at a weekend soccer tournament. Shouldn't we plan just as well in case something tragic happens to either of us? After all, if I can't manage a weekend without an instruction list, how easy would it be for either of us to manage the loss of the other, and wouldn't some guidance to help us through the transition be helpful?

Dianne and I both hope to be around for a long, long time, but if we didn't plan for the possibility that we might not be here at some point, I know I would not be doing right by Dianne and our daughters (and evidently Shelby). Our children are still young enough that they're not involved in that process with us, but they're not too many years away from the beginnings of those conversations.

Those are tough talks. I know attorneys who have yet to draft their own wills, and that is likely because of how hard it is to broach these matters with their own families. Still, it is essential. Many people have put off doing proper estate planning, or if they have done so, they haven't talked it over with their spouse. They do what they believe is in the best interest of the spouse, who may even have signed the papers, but there hasn't really been a conversation of any depth. In fact, this can be a source of frustration between spouses. Not many people want to enter into an agreement unknowingly, even when they trust the other party and agree with the principles and the rationale.

Often, my role is to be the third party in the room. I can facilitate those kinds of conversations and help couples bring up issues that they otherwise might never mention. I can also help to coordinate the conversations with their lawyers and CPAs, depending on what needs to be accomplished. Very often, I'm the one who initiates the conversations (sometimes by giving them a book to read, as a less-than-subtle hint). If you aren't having these conversations currently, approach your current team about who wants to take the lead on these discussions and coordinate. Normally, once they know you are interested, there will be at least one team member who is willing to step up to the plate and has probably even been unsuccessfully trying to engage you in these conversations all along. If you don't have that teammate, it might be time to adjust your team or find a new member.

THE LOVING THING TO DO

What you don't want is for the family to be in utter disarray upon a death regardless if that person managed the purse strings or the heartstrings. And yet this is common, and it is unfortunate. This should be a time of grieving, not scrambling around. It should be a time for hearts to heal.

The attitude is often, "We'll get around to this; there's plenty of time." And then that time runs short and ends. Someone has a stroke, Alzheimer's sets in, or a car crashes on the highway. We just don't know, and yet many people live as if it couldn't happen—as if they are invincible.

Planning is relatively easy to do, but you have to get started. It's a pleasure to plan for the good and positive things in life, but you also need to make provisions for the people you care about. They must be prepared for a day when you might not be there for them.

Some of these concerns can be handled quite readily. For example, it's simple and straightforward to let your spouse know where to find the will. Surprisingly often, a surviving spouse who signed the will has no idea where it is located. Often the survivor has little or no idea about assets or real estate holdings and does not even know the online passwords to access information. It would not have taken much advance planning to avoid those headaches. At the very least, the family should know whom to contact and where to get information to start the process.

It's hard enough to be heartbroken at your spouse's funeral. Why be worried sick, too? Advance planning will not ease the pain of your loss, but it will ease the burden of financial pressures and lessen one type of stress. The solution is careful and thorough financial planning that involves both spouses and possibly their children. Such planning can be simple, such as providing those passwords; it can be thoughtful, such as funeral planning; and it can be complicated, such as comprehensive estate and business transition planning.

It's not my purpose here to get into the details, but families should certainly do so during their discussions. Your loved ones should be feeling thankful that you were part of their life, not anxious about all they have to do in your absence.

CHAPTER 6
THE WISE WIDOW/WIDOWER

First, take a deep breath

W hen the inevitable happens and your spouse passes, you will have some matters to take care of—and the length of the list and the complexity of the tasks will depend upon how well you have planned together.

But no matter how well you have planned, you probably didn't think of everything. You still will have some matters, hopefully small ones, to deal with. With a few discussions and a little planning, you can avoid some of the basic issues that are more stressful than people realize. Wouldn't it be easier if you did not have to worry about where to find all those documents, choosing an executor, visiting with the lawyers, and going through the probate process? All of those things can be addressed in advance so that they are not pressing upon you in your immediate time of grief. If you didn't do it, do not despair—but it is likely that you will soon find yourself advising others to get these matters out of the way without delay.

No matter how much or how little planning you have done, you should take these basic steps first:

1. Before anything, take a deep breath.

2. Do not make any rash decisions.

3. Your immediate concerns should not be financial ones. You have time to make decisions, and sometimes, taking action too soon will limit your choices. If in doubt, refer to items one and two.

4. Reach out for the support of family and friends to help you get through the funeral. This is a time to draw close to family.

5. Reach out to your financial team. They should be able to do much of the heavy financial lifting for you while you work on the more important personal issues.

Just remember there should be time enough in the weeks and months to come to move forward. In these emotional times, it is especially easy to make poor financial decisions, so always refer back to items one and two.

A TEAM ON YOUR SIDE

Ideally, you will have a trusted team with whom you have been working and who can coordinate the financial issues as they come up. What your team should not be doing is pushing you to make decisions that you are not quite ready to make. If you do not have a team in place, do not feel rushed to deal with the first person you talk to or with the family friend who may or may not be fully qualified to help you. Take the time to interview some folks to find the ones who are good fits for you and with whom you feel comfortable. I can't stress how important it is to feel comfortable with your team. If you don't, move on. There are plenty of capable advisors in this world, and this isn't the time to settle or stay in a relationship you aren't comfortable with.

You may find that the advisor with whom your spouse was working is simply not someone who is a match for you. If that's the case, that's okay. You need to move ahead with the advisor who suits you best. You may never have even met your spouse's team members, so rest assured that he or she would want you to be at ease with whomever you are trusting with your financial matters.

Making sure you have the right team is your first and most important financial task. You should not commit to any financial decisions before you have that team in place, and you should give yourself some time to let everything settle and to go through the grieving process. You will need to find out your

> "I can't stress how important it is to feel comfortable with your team."

options, and when the time comes that you must make those choices, you can do so with a level head and the expert support of people you know and trust. That is how you move forward in an empowered position.

Dianne has been introduced to some of the people we call our "financial board of directors." She has met our estate lawyer and accountant, for example, and before we retained them, we talked about whether they were a good fit. She had veto power over them. After all, if something were to happen to me, this team would be her first line of defense. It only makes sense that she should know them in advance and already have trust and confidence in them.

Dianne also knows who is on my short list of financial planners I trust. So if I were to die or become incapacitated, she knows who I would want to manage the family money and help her with the next stage of financial planning. We have had those discussions. Besides, I'm fortunate to have a team practice, and I have introduced her to people I trust.

Trust and competence are the two big factors. Your advisor certainly needs to possess the know-how and experience to serve you well, but that person can hardly do so if you would rather be dealing with somebody else. You deserve respect from an advisor, and he or she should seek out the opinions of both spouses, even if one is taking the clear lead in the discussions. If you feel left out of the conversations, you may feel similarly disenfranchised someday when you are meeting with that person alone.

That is why I have gone out of my way to be sure that Dianne is familiar with the people she is likely to work with someday. That will give her the confidence to hand over management of her affairs to them, if need be. For example, she has met Keith, our CPA®, and would be able to work with him each year as he guides her through the information he needs at tax time. She knows that if accounting issues were to arise, he would be there for her.

When you are grieving, you need the reassurance that competent hands will be handling your financial matters. You do not necessarily need to know the details, but you do need to know that the one you love trusted these people and cared enough to introduce you so that you might trust them, too. While that means a lot, it is not every-thing. You still might find the need to switch to a different advisor. Sometimes it's just a personality clash. You might just not click. Or sometimes the style with which one spouse works with an advisor is different than the surviving spouses. Only you know when the relationship is working.

SO MANY QUESTIONS

When you are facing the years ahead without the one who had long handled the family's financial affairs, you will certainly have many questions. Chief among them will be how in the world will you handle all of these financial affairs? If you already were responsible for much of that aspect of your marriage, then for that portion of life, it might just seem like business as usual. For many, though, finance is a whole new world.

If you are older, you and your spouse might already have begun some of the transfer of assets to future generations. If that is unfamiliar ground to you, then your team can help you manage those aspects while you continue to take care of the financial duties that you know how to do. An experienced team will simplify matters for you. You need that experience, and if you do not yet possess it yourself, this is not the time to practice.

Nor should you be letting others without experience handle your affairs. That includes family. I have seen children trying to help their parents, or their surviving parent, make good decisions. Their intentions may be good, but the advice might not be in anyone's best interest—and their suggestions might not be possible or even legal. Often, they just end up complicating matters. Family members can be great support, and I encourage them to be involved in the process, but if they have questions it is best for you to meet with your advisors as a family so all aspects of a situation can be addressed. Remember, no matter who is putting pressure on you to do something, start by taking a deep breath, and relax as best you can because you still have to maintain the leadership role lest the decisions become tilted in unintended directions.

Also don't get too frustrated with the small matters that can be quickly addressed. For example, I know that one issue Dianne and I still need to address is getting her car in her own name. The only reason it is in my name is that on the day we got it, she had to take the girls to soccer practice and couldn't come with me to the dealership to sign the papers. The trouble is that if I were to pass away, the car would have to go through the estate process. A simple fix now could avoid hassles later. But if we never get around to dealing with it (hopefully I outlive the car), it is an easy fix based on our estate plan.

This is partially true because we have already selected our executor. Couples need to decide upon an executor for the estate, whether it is the surviving spouse or someone else. That person will be responsible for such things as getting assets properly titled for probate. For example, the house deed would need to be changed to an individual name, in addition to dealing with the status of personal property such as the car.

We decided to use a corporate executor because frankly, having seen and dealt with that process, I would not wish it on my worst enemy. I certainly would not want Dianne or one of my children to face that burden and those potentially painful decisions. We decided that a third party—a corporate trustee—would be the best choice so that we could stay out of the probate process as much as possible and deal more with the grief of loss than with the grief of dealing with a probate court.

The executor will be in charge of tracking down information on probate assets and continuing to monitor that information. Often tasks like this can be more complicated than we imagine. For example, collecting rents on rental property can be a difficult task when a spouse takes over, particularly one who has not been involved in running the family business. It amazes me how people who owe money to the business will simply stop paying the family during its time of sorrow—this frequently happens with renters of real estate. Perhaps they think the surviving spouse might not have the heart to ask for the money at that stage. That's another reason to go with a corporate trustee or executor who can step into that role.

Those are just some examples of the many issues, small and big, that can come up during this time. Each issue and concept has to be taken one at a time. What it comes down to is that a lot of these things can be handled better before the fact than after. However, if they haven't been handled, there's still a lot that can be done once a good team is in place. That is why I place so much emphasis on getting to know those folks. Life will proceed much more smoothly if you are assured of competent assistance in the transition and if you take care of a lot of the details in advance.

SECTION TWO REVIEW

This section of the book has dealt primarily with issues that involve anticipating the death of a loved one. Let's take a look at some things we have learned and consider some steps you might take when faced with those circumstances.

When your spouse passes away, take a deep breath. A lot is happening. This is a time to reach out to people with whom you can share the burden, whether they are friends, family, or professionals. You need time to grieve.

Many things can wait, but some things need immediate attention. Arrange for organ donation if that was a wish. This, of course, will need to be an immediate decision. Notify immediate family. You can ask them for help in notifying other friends and family. Do not try to call everyone yourself. If the body is to be bequeathed to a medical hospital, make arrangements. That decision may well have been put in writing in advance, but even if it was not, this can still be accomplished.

Now, take another deep breath. In the next few days, you can plan for the funeral.

Whenever possible, involve key family members in this decision process. The wishes may already be known, and in that case (if the wishes were reasonable), follow what has been previously decided. Otherwise, think about what the deceased would have wanted and what will help the family the most. Move forward from there.

You may already have a funeral home selected; if so, contact them. They can help with most of what needs to be done and will generally have some form of checklist that will help you through the process. Another great resource for a checklist is AARP. A checklist helps to keep track of what needs to be done by you, and you can use it to identify items that you may be able to delegate to others. Then you can use it to track the responsibilities you have delegated and to whom and the items you have already accomplished. I strongly recommend the use of a checklist as a means to keep items organized at a difficult time like this.

In the upcoming days, you will need to start pulling information together. Here is a short list of documents, if available, that you may need or that could come in handy.

- multiple copies of the death certificate—you will need more than you think
- Social Security card
- birth certificate
- marriage certificate
- deeds and titles to property (including car registrations)
- insurance policies
- stock certificates
- bonds
- bank books (quickly becoming a thing of the past)
- loans
- honorable discharge papers or VA claim number
- anything that comes on a statement

SECTION THREE
FATHERLY ADVICE

Dear Katelyn and Larissa,

I don't want to write this letter, because it means that I wasn't there to see you through this part of your life. These are the things that I had hoped to teach you either by word or by deed. My hope here is to fill in at least the gaps of what I was unable to share.

First, note that I have faith and confidence in both of you and know that you have good heads on your shoulders. Second, know that you are going to mess up at some point and make mistakes, and they probably will be painful. The good news is that later you will see that some of those mistakes led to your success—or at least they will give you a few laughs. They will be "exquisite mistakes," in the words of Harpeth Hall headmaster Stephanie Balmer.

Girls, always be learning. Take risks, and do your best. Make those exquisite mistakes, and then take responsibility for them. Cry, if necessary, learn from them, and then laugh (after all it is the best medicine)—just try not to repeat them.

"Each of you is perfect the way you are—and you can use a little improvement."

SHUNRYU SUZUKI

CHAPTER 7
THE SAVVY SINGLE

What you someday may wish you had known

I write the words to this chapter thinking of our two young daughters and all the dreams and hopes that Dianne and I have for them. I hope to be here for them as the years go by and share in their joys and challenges as they grow and launch into life. And yet I know that there is a possibility that our time together could be cut short. Tomorrow is never certain for anyone.

I hope that one day they will start their own families, in which case they will be making decisions jointly with their spouses. As a couple starting out, they will find a lot of good advice in the first section of this book. But our children, like most, will certainly be spending some time as single adults as well, and I want them to be equipped with the skills to move forward independently in life.

I think about what I would wish to tell them and what I would want them to understand if I were not there to say it in person. My fatherly advice would cover a wide range of topics. When it comes to money, however, I think the first thing that I would want them to know is that money is merely a tool. It must be used responsibly to attain the things that are important in life. It does not define you. You define what you do with it.

Money is a means to freedom, and you must not be enslaved to it. That is the attitude that I would hope they would carry with them throughout their lives.

People who inherit a substantial sum of money have a responsibility to be good stewards of those dollars. They should manage the money appropriately. It needs to be used for the benefit of others as well as oneself, and it should be nurtured so that it can

> "Money is a means to freedom, and you must not be enslaved to it."

grow to benefit the generation that follows. Many inheritors are afraid to take even small risks to grow their inheritance, but for wealth to be sustainable across time and generations, growth is a necessity.

If you are fortunate enough to have investments and savings or an inheritance, then you should think about using it as a tool for good. You should set goals for your life that you want the money to help you achieve. And when your days are done, if you've been a good steward, you may have as much or more money to leave to each of your children independently as was left to you.

So much depends on developing good habits involving finances, as with all else in life. If you develop the habit of living within your means and saving your money, you will be happier. Many have testified to the truth of that principle. It's not about how much money you make but how you adapt that money to your lifestyle.

Dianne and I hope to leave our children a legacy that they will continue—an inheritance of money, yes, but also a legacy of good works that they can do in this world. We hope that someday they will be telling another generation about what their parents and grandparents accomplished.

A SUMMARY OF ESSENTIALS

Some of the advice that I would give to my children is very simple, but I cannot highlight it enough. Here are some of the essentials:

- Do not spend more than you make. Always save a portion of your income so that it can build toward a prosperous future. Do not buy things for status. You should buy things because they bring you joy or are useful to you, not because you think they make you look important. Most things like that are not worth owning. And no matter how much you have, always be productive. Always add value and be a "net giver" instead of subtracting value and being a "net taker."

- Do not fall into the trap of stupid debt. Debt can be a phenomenal tool to leverage and to provide positive arbitrage, but it can also be very dangerous. A good rule of thumb is that you should never take on debt for something that will not last as long as the debt itself. Understand the difference between good debt and bad debt. If you pay for a meal today on a credit card that you will not repay for months, you are accepting bad debt. If you buy a house that you are confident will appreciate in value as you live in it over the years, you are probably taking on good debt.

- So many young people, when they leave home and get their first job, expect that they will be living a lifestyle similar to that of their parents. What you should expect instead is that you will grow into that kind of lifestyle, presuming it was a comfortable one. It is important when you are starting out that you appreciate the value of the dollars that come your way so that you do not fall victim to a sense of entitlement. Adopt a humble attitude as you strive to make the most of your situation, but don't try to make it more than it is. Even though my parents paid for my college education, in many ways I was a poor college student and still had to live within a tight budget. Those were important lessons.

- Money is meant to be managed. That is true whether you are simply paying your bills or are overseeing elaborate investments. You need to know the essentials of sound money management, even if at times you delegate some of those tasks to professionals. You never want to get to the point where you feel like the money is managing you. Again, money is a tool with which you should aspire to do great things in the world. It should not be making you miserable.

- Know why you are doing what you do. If you think of your finances as a business that you are running, keep in mind that all businesses should have goals and priorities. What are your long-term desires for the money that you are setting aside? Never lose sight of that. You have a purpose and a dream. Over time, your dreams may change, so you'll need to reset your sights and keep on going. You need that goal. Otherwise, how will you achieve anything? You need to define for yourself what success will look like.

- Control your money. Do not let it control you. That's a good rule for life itself. Do not let stuff just happen to you. Be the one to make things happen. Just as money is meant to be managed, so is your life. How are you managing your health? How are you managing your relationships? How are you holding fast to your values? People who have good habits in one area tend to have good habits in other areas. If you lack good money habits, it is likely that you also will not be eating right, exercising enough, or cultivating good relationships.

- Do not be fooled: money matters, even if people are fond of saying otherwise. It matters because of what it signifies. It represents our efforts to make our way in this world. It symbolizes our ability to reach for a brighter future. Anyone who says that money doesn't matter has never truly gone without money. It is no sin to be poor. In fact, I think most people would benefit from that condition for a period of their lives. It can provide a much-needed perspective. You learn the value of working hard toward something better. You are very fortunate as an American with a great education, being poor would be a choice, but most of the world isn't as privileged as you are. Feel free to make that choice, but if you do, please do something meaningful with your life. For example, a teacher elects to never create great wealth through their income, but their job symbolizes an investment in our society. Decide which is best: to earn money and use it as a tool to improve the world or to forgo wealth and be an element for change yourself. There is value in both.

- Learn how you can build value and exchange that value for other things. You may grow up to make a fortune, or you may earn relatively little, but you need to be comfortable and happy and understand that, regardless of how much you make, you need to be good stewards of those dollars.

- Always be learning. It is no secret that I place a lot of value on education. I have my master's degree and multiple designations, and I will continue to take classes for the rest of my life. When I am not taking a class, I am reading— probably more than you realize. You can never go wrong when you are investing in your own abilities. However, I do believe that you should always assess the expected return on your education investment. It makes little sense to get a college degree in something that you can't turn into a job or profession. Once you have an education that can provide you with a living, I also am a firm believer in education for its own sake, as a *luxury*. There is a place for that type of education as well—just be sure you know the difference. You need to balance the costs and attain the specific education that will advance your career first. Through it all, though, you should be embracing the love of learning. Ultimately, that is what will bring you the greatest return as you enrich your life and the lives of those you touch.

MAKE SAVINGS A HABIT

As a young person starting out, you may be thinking that there are one or two more things you need or another luxury that a friend has that you don't. Well, get over it! If all your friends do is buy things instead of save for their future, they will be poor their entire lives. Start saving now so that won't be you. It's that simple.

A dollar saved and invested at a hypothetical 12 percent works out to roughly $3 that you won't have to save in ten years, $9 that you won't have to save in twenty years, $30 that you won't have to save in thirty years, and $90 you won't have to save in forty years. No little trinket you buy today will be worth what you will eventually have.

Budgeting means nothing more than knowing your exact income and expenses and having a plan for managing your money. It's very difficult to stick to your financial goals without a budget because you'll be driven more by momentary needs and desires. I can't stress enough how important it is to have a plan and to start saving on a regular basis—for life. Early in our marriage, the most difficult times Dianne and I had involved financial stress. We were fortunate compared to the many couples who don't survive financial stress. After all, it is one of the leading causes of divorce and can even contribute to health problems.

So take responsibility, and take that first step in your own financial well-being. For most beginners, the first step to financial well-being is to keep a healthy cash reserve as your first defense against life's mishaps. Three months of expenses for many people may seem like a tremendous amount of idle cash, especially when you are living paycheck to paycheck. However, it really is only the starting point of where your reserve should be. Remember, if something can go wrong, as Murphy's Law says, it will—so be prepared.

The important thing is to just get started. (Yes, I know I am repeating myself, but that is how important getting started actually is.) Once you do get started, keep your savings in a separate account that isn't regularly accessed or even seen. The rule of thumb and basic human nature is if you don't see it, you won't spend it! So hide it. The best place to keep your cash reserve and any other savings is as far from your checking account as possible. People tend to spend everything that is in their checking account because it is so readily available.

> **"The important thing is to just get started."**

So separate all savings (not just the cash reserve) from your monthly expenditures. Only move money out of savings when you are making a large and necessary purchase you planned for or in an emergency, and don't move more than you have budgeted.

The other great benefit of structuring your savings outside of your checking account is that you can earn additional interest. One simple way to do this is by keeping your first month's reserve in cash and your next two to three months in rolling CDs or even short-term government bonds. For savings beyond three month's income, you may even try low-risk bond funds and very conservative balanced funds.

This way, you still maintain access to funds when you need them. The majority of your reserve is principle-protected, but at least you have an opportunity to get a little growth. Hopefully you will never have an incident that requires you to use all of your cash reserve, but even if you do, it should be infrequent enough that the costs of market gyrations are outweighed by time in the market. If you are reaching into your reserves more frequently or so deeply to reach beyond three month's income than they aren't really cash reserves at all and you need to review your budget.

The one thing I must stress is that your cash reserve is not designed to hold high-risk dollars. You are looking for investments that carry little or no risk. Make sure that whomever you are working with knows that you may need these dollars at any time. Smaller fluctuations and easy access are more important than large gains because these are the dollars you call on when things go wrong. Remember, a recession can cause both the loss of a job and the stock market to decline, so don't take risks with your cash reserve no matter what returns you are promised.

A question I am frequently asked is whether one should use a cash reserve to make a big purchase, like a car. The answer is no; your cash reserve is for emergencies and unforeseen events only. You need to save specifically for other big-ticket items, like a car, because if you do not, then every time your cash reserve hits a certain point, you will go out and purchase a new car, sending your cash reserve back to zero!

Saving for a new car and investing in a cash reserve do not mean that you have to have a separate account for both. It just means that you always leave a minimum of three months expenses in your reserves that you cannot dip into unless there is an emergency. Beyond that number, money may be used for planned expenditures like a vacation, a new car, or a down payment on your next home.

The good news is that, with a little discipline, most savers have saved enough to cover any big-ticket item sooner than they expect. If this is the case, it is time to diversify your portfolio beyond the cash reserve and into more growth-oriented positions. The important thing to remember is that even if all of these dollars are in the same account, you need to be able to differentiate between investments comprising your cash reserve and investments earmarked for the long term. If you haven't allocated them this way, you are probably taking too much or too little risk.

INVESTMENT BASICS

You also need to be investing for your retirement. As you probably know, you cannot depend upon Social Security for all of your needs, so let's look at some investment basics. The two most common approaches to investing are lump sum and dollar-cost averaging (DCA).

LUMP-SUM APPROACH

The name alone tells you that this isn't for everyone. To invest a lump sum, you actually need the lump to begin with. If you do not have tons of cash just sitting around to invest, then you can't be a lump-sum investor. One of the reasons you may have a lump sum to invest is because you have come into a large windfall of cash—an inheritance, for example, or a big bonus.

Once you have cash beyond your cash reserve (and savings for large purchases), your money needs to be invested for the long haul. If you can handle the risk, some or all of it should be invested in equities. As a general rule, you are better off getting your money into the market sooner rather than later because the longer you are in the market, the more upside opportunity is available to you. The one exception is the summer months, which historically have been the worst period of the year for the stock market. In that case, waiting until fall may work to your advantage, although that isn't the case every year.

DCA APPROACH[4]

For most people, DCA is the way you have to start (because you simply don't have a lump sum). An example of this is if you are participating in your company's retirement plan, you already invest monthly (or per pay period) into 401(k)s because you really have no other choice. Your income comes in a paycheck, normally monthly or bimonthly, so your saving happens in this time frame as well. Another example most people don't think are bonuses or tax refunds. They think of them as lump-sum investments, but what they don't realize is if every year you invest an annual bonus or your tax refund, it still counts as DCA. You are just doing it annually instead of monthly.

The reality for the average young investor is that you will probably be putting your dollars into the market as quickly as possible by following some combination of payroll withholding and monthly investing. And investing as quickly as possible makes sense if we assume that the market generally increases over time and that it goes up more often than it goes down; doesn't it make sense to invest in it as quickly as possible? And that automatic, no matter what, factor of setting up a DCA is what makes it an ideal way to start investing.

After all, it is important that you do not believe the hype of trying to time the market. The reality is that the faster the money goes into the market, the longer it has to grow. If you wait to make a large investment, then you may miss a period of growth in the stock market while you let your cash sit on the sidelines. In other words, the main reason to DCA is not to play the minor, month-to-month market fluctuations but to get the money into the market as fast as

---

4 Regular investing does not assure a profit or protect against a loss in declining markets. Dollar-cost averaging involves continuous investments in securities regardless of fluctuating price levels. Investors should consider their financial ability to continue purchases through periods of low price levels.

possible because the odds are more in your favor every additional day your money is invested.

DCA is simply the way to save so that someday you will have large lump sums to invest. Now that you know that you have to DCA, where do you do it?

QUALIFIED PROGRAMS

Better known as *retirement plans*, qualified plans are what the IRS and the federal government officially recognize as tax-preferred methods of saving for retirement. If your investment has a special tax treatment and you have to tell the IRS how much you put in and take out each year, then it is a qualified plan. Another way to identify a plan that could be considered qualified is if there are penalties for taking your money out too soon (before age fifty-nine and a half); or if you take it out too late (after age seventy and a half).

In plain English, any time you have money in a qualified program, there are strings attached. The most well-known qualified plan in today's world is the 401(k). The basics of the program are pretty simple. The IRS allows you, in cooperation with your employer, to put a certain percentage of your income into a specified group of investments before the money is taxed and before the money makes it into your checking account. In addition, they also allow your employer to put money into the accounts on your behalf, free of current income tax. The catch? In this case, you are taxed when

> "In plain English, any time you have money in a qualified program, there are strings attached."

you withdraw the money, and it is all treated as income and taxable at your income rate.

This creates two issues. First, the IRS limits your access to the money. And second, for many people in the highest income tax brackets, it becomes a bit of a trap. Think of it this way: when you are young, you have tax deductions such as children, mortgage interest, and maybe contributions to an IRA. However, when you retire, you probably have fewer deductions, so your tax bracket may be unchanged (or even higher, if your income increased throughout your life). Or another way to put it is if your goal is to substantially increase your lifestyle as you get older, that may also mean you have increased your income and are now paying income taxes at a higher rate than when you first graduated from college. Basically, after a long and successful career you retire and want to maintain the same lifestyle you had right before you retired, and your tax rate probably won't change. Especially since you will be taxed on the withdrawals you make from certain retirement accounts like the 401(k) or traditional IRA. So if you only have tax-deferred accounts to pull income from, you may be taxed at a higher rate on those dollars than you would have been when you initially put them into the account (right after college). This means that unless you cut your retirement lifestyle, you will at the very least maintain your last tax rate.

This is the point when most people ask whether they should even contribute to a 401(k). The answer is that you definitely should—especially if you are receiving a match. You should always invest at least up to that point. After that, it gets a little more complicated, and you need to consider your income level and how much you are saving elsewhere.

So before we max out the traditional 401(k), let's look at what other options are available.

ROTH IRA

For most people, the best retirement option—after they have maxed out their company's traditional 401(k) match—is the Roth IRA. (This assumes that your adjusted gross income is under the threshold; this changes almost every year, so check with your tax advisor). The Roth IRA is the opposite of the traditional 401(k). With the traditional 401(k), you get all of the tax breaks up front; your income is tax-deferred going into the account and turns into taxable income coming out. With the Roth, you pay income taxes on the money you deposit into the account as you normally would. But when you pull the money out, after age fifty-nine and a half, the growth is tax-free.

Let's assume you put the money into the account in 2009, and the law that year allowed a maximum investment of $5,000 with a catch-up provision of an additional $1,000 if you are over age fifty. For my clients who were having an off year, this was a dream come true. Why? Because when you go to take the money out, as long as you are over the age of fifty-nine and a half, no taxes are due. This is one of the reasons that the IRS limits the amount you can put in.

Where do I tell my clients to put their money? First, invest in the 401(k) to the maximum; nothing beats free money from your employer. Next, if you are eligible, max out your Roth IRA. Once you have done that, go back to the 401(k) and put as much into it as you can afford. You should shoot to have a minimum of 10 percent of your salary deferred every year in IRAs or 401(k)s.

An option that has been around for a while but that employers are only now starting to adopt is the Roth option on the 401(k). You get the tax benefits of a Roth IRA with the potential matching of a traditional 401(k). If you have this option and are expecting your tax brackets to go up in the future, utilize this option first.

TRADITIONAL IRA

The traditional IRA works similarly to the 401(k) except that there is no match and the money generally hits your checking account first. You then invest it and get your write-off at the end of the year. Because there is no match, go with the 401(k) first. At that point, it becomes a question of whether you want to contribute to a traditional IRA or a Roth IRA. The guidelines for the traditional IRAs are more restrictive, and unless you are certain you are going to be in a lower tax bracket in retirement, stick with the Roth IRA, even if you are eligible to participate in the traditional IRA.

The reason that most of my clients end up with the traditional IRA is that when you separate from your employer, you can roll over the old 401(k) into a traditional IRA, which allows greater control and more investment choices.

NONQUALIFIED ACCOUNTS

Nonqualified accounts generally offer little or no tax advantage, but they do offer more access to the assets and investment flexibility. Following are some examples of different types of nonqualified accounts.

SAVINGS ACCOUNTS

These earn interest, have little risk, and allow you easy access to your money. Money market accounts also fall into this category. The downside of these accounts is that your returns are normally muted and you get taxed on the income every year. These are not retirement accounts (or at least, they should not be). They are cash reserves or savings for any large purchase that you may need to make in the next five years.

Otherwise, you should invest your money for the longer term. Whenever you are putting money aside for a rainy day or a large purchase and are more concerned about accessibility than growth, a savings account is the way to go.

INVESTMENT ACCOUNTS

After you leave the low-risk, low-return saving accounts, the field of investments, tax treatments, *and* the levels of risk open up. You can open investment accounts with a variety of securities, depending on your purposes. You may choose to invest in federal, municipal, or corporate bonds. Individual equities, better known as stocks, are another option. However, they carry much greater short-term risk, but they also have the potential for greater long-term rewards such as dividend yields and some deferral of taxable gain until you sell the asset. Mutual funds and exchange-traded funds (ETFs) are baskets of stock, bonds, and even other alternative publicly traded assets. It is important that before you purchase any of these investments you do the research since their underlying assets and risk can vary significantly.

For convenience and diversification needs, most people start out investing in open-ended mutual funds. Most mutual fund companies will allow you to start with as little as $100 on a monthly draft or with a single lump sum of $2,000. There are a number of well-known companies, like Morningstar, that can assist you with making good choices. But remember that even if a fund has done well in the past, it may not be appropriate for you, and it may not continue its success into the future.

Mutual funds can be purchased in a variety of ways. The choice is dependent on how active you want to be in the decision-making process, how much risk you want to take, how much time you want to spend on your investments, and whether you are set on going it alone or would prefer professional advice.

AVOIDING THE CREDIT CARD TRAP

As you become established professionally and personally, you may go through a period where you desperately want to play the game of "trying to keep up with the Joneses" and develop an affinity, or possibly an addiction, for consumer goods. This is also the point when many recent graduates first encounter debt other than student loans. But as with everything in life, the key is to find a balance. So here are some rules about credit cards. I try to avoid blanket statements, but here is one anyway: *Credit cards are dangerous!* Here is why.

You spend more. Picture yourself going to a convenience store to buy gum, only to realize that you are fifteen cents short. Rather than walking out to the car to scrounge some change, you pull out your credit card. However, you need to meet the minimum purchase to use the card, so you buy a soda, some chips, and perhaps a few items you see on the counter. Not only do you spend more and wreck your budget, you also buy a bunch of unhealthy food and gain weight. I said they were dangerous, but maybe I should amend that to evil—spend more money and gain weight, if that isn't evil . . .

Research shows that when a person uses a credit card instead of cash, their spending goes up between 12 and 18 percent on average.[5] This is true whether you are at the convenience store or buying furniture. Of course, the furniture store loves it when you sign up for their card. *Do you really think they are giving you a bargain if they offer you 10 percent off of your first purchase and no payments until the new millennium?* They do it because they know you are going to buy not only the couch (which you may have had enough cash to pay for immediately) but also a couple of extras, like those throw pillows that match perfectly and a side table, which of course needs a lamp too.

So the amount of money you were planning on spending has now doubled. The furniture store is also banking on the fact that you are going to be the typical consumer and not quite have everything paid off by the end of the free interest period (which probably won't last until the new millennium—I may have exaggerated that one just a bit). Not to mention that the average consumer seldom gets everything paid off by the end of the term, which makes this a great deal for them—you spent twice as much as you planned, and now you are paying a ridiculously high interest rate to boot.

However, if I can't convince you to completely avoid credit card debt, you can at least make some smart moves of your own. Start by following these two simple rules of consumer debt. The first one is this: Whatever you buy should be paid off before you finish using it. And here's the second: Always refer to rule number one.

Let's look at some quick examples. If you go out to dinner, pay with cash. A trip to the movies? Pay with cash. Going to a football game? Pay with cash once again. The same holds true for groceries,

---

5 Bill Hardekopf, "Credit Card Tips for Holiday Shopping," Forbes, November, 12, 2010, http://www.forbes.com/sites/moneybuilder/2010/11/12/credit-card-tips-for-holiday-shopping/#7625b2cf751f.

gas, clothes, or anything that will no longer be of use once the bill arrives.

Understandably, some big-ticket items like cars (especially early in your career) may cause you to take on some debt. However, you still need to plan to have the car paid off before getting your next car. If you cannot do so, then you are looking at a car that is too expensive for your budget.

If you do succumb to the dark side and utilize a credit card, follow these rules to limit the damage as much as possible.

The four rules for your credit card:

1. Every time you make a purchase, immediately transfer money from your checking account to your credit card. This way you can use your credit card like you would an ATM card. With online bill pay, it is easy. You also avoid unpleasant surprises in the mail by using this technique. But best of all, it will force you to look at your checking account when you make the transfer, making you more aware of your current balance.

2. If you are trying to earn points or cash back, you can use your credit card for ongoing bills that you know you are going to have every month, like your cell phone. You can then set up your bill pay to send a check to the credit card company to pay off that portion of your bill automatically.

3. Pay your credit card off every month. Do so even if you have to dip into savings. Once you start carrying a balance, it becomes easier and easier to rationalize larger and larger balances, so make the sacrifice and dip into savings. This is true even if the credit card company is offering you zero percent interest. Their hope is that you will be so used to

carrying the balance that when the rate does go up, you either will not notice or will lack the cash to pay it off.

4. Use your credit card for reimbursable business expenses. Your company should reimburse you before the bill is due. Then just transfer the entire amount of the reimbursement check to the credit card company. Try to use a separate card for this purpose. That way, you can make certain that you are in balance every month and you don't have to worry about picking personal expenses out of the business ones. You get the points; they get the bill.

If you have already succumbed to the credit bug, it's time for immediate action! Remove your credit cards from your wallet or purse, and leave them at home. If you are already carrying credit card debt, this is the first debt you need to pay off. If possible, move the balances to the cards with the lowest rates and then aggressively pay the debt down. Make no big purchases while you have credit card debt, and that includes planning vacations.

BUYING YOUR FIRST CAR

For many, their first big ticket purchase is a car. The most common question is whether to buy new or used. If we look at some simple math, the answer is pretty obvious. Everyone, or at least almost everyone, has heard that a car drops in value as soon as you drive it off the lot. With most cars, this depreciation is actually in the range of 20 percent and happens as soon as the purchase is final (in some states there is a two-day look back period from date of signature). If you doubt this, try and sell the car back to the dealer and see if they will give you what you paid for it.

What most people don't realize is that if you take care of your car, the best time to sell it is not when the wheels are about to fall off but normally just before the car turns five. Most people can't tell the difference between cars that are one and two years old. However, when a car is over five years of age, there probably has been a model change, there may be a few more dings, and it is no longer considered a late model and instead considered "older."

Older cars have several things that detract from their value for a couple of years past that five-year mark. First, they normally have higher financing costs. Then factor in that they also probably have more mileage and in the new car lot there is that shiny new body style just sitting in the showroom waiting for you, and you can begin to understand why they might depreciate faster for a couple of years. But after a couple more years (normally beginning around year seven) depreciation begins to slow down considerably.

If you make the good decision to shop for a used car rather than a new car, you need to determine whether you want a slightly used, late-model vehicle or something older. Remember that burst of depreciation around the five-year mark? That often makes cars that are seven-plus years old a bargain. They potentially have a few more mechanical problems than a newer model, but the lower cost can more than make up for it. Remember that most of today's cars can easily run between 150,000 and 200,000 miles before there are serious mechanical issues.

Look at your budget and at what you want to buy. If you are desperate for that new car look and can afford it, then buy a one-year-old car and replace it every three to four years. If you do just this, you are ahead of the average consumer.

However, if you want the absolute best deal, you need to identify a car model that has just undergone a major body style change and look for a low-mileage specimen of the previous body style—preferably in the four- to six-year-old range. The body style change results in faster depreciation of the older model, which means you get a bargain.

Even if you choose not to go with the older models and instead stick with the late-model car that you sell by year five, the savings can be enormous. Let's assume you are a two-car family that replaces each car every five years. You would end up with roughly $40,000 in savings between just your twentieth and thirtieth birthdays by skipping the new car lot. If you then invest that $40,000 until your retirement at age sixty-five, assuming a 10 percent return over thirty-five years, you would have approximately $1,124,097 more saved for retirement.

How many people realize that buying a couple of new cars in their twenties could have cost them over $1 million in retirement savings?

And if you are willing to give up a couple of those prestige points and drive the slightly older body style, you can probably double your savings. Another common question is whether you should lease or purchase. In today's world, you can still lease, finance, or pay cash. Depending upon your situation, any of the three may work.

> "And if you are willing to give up a couple of those prestige points and drive the slightly older body style, you can probably double your savings."

First, let's look at the cash option. Generally speaking, and in a perfect world, this is the best. The fact is that you should not buy a car until you can pay cash for it. In other words, you should keep driving your old car until you have cash to pay for a new car.

However, having worked with young professionals, I know the odds of you pulling up to your new office in a jalopy are slim. Anyway, even if you have the cash to pay for the car, always compare all three options and get a quote for each. A dealership may offer you different prices or deals based upon your financing choice. So check that first. Next, see if they are running any specials on interest rates.

The factors to look at when you decide between leasing and normal financing are a little more complicated. But unless you are going to trade your car in every two or three years with very low mileage, you probably do not have a chance of winning with leasing—that is, unless you are a small business and can take advantage of the tax write-offs. Even in this situation, most accountants will tell you that leasing is the worst of your three options.

In short, here is what I recommend:

1. Buy used.
2. Compare all three options (cash, loan, and lease).
3. Whenever possible, pay cash.
4. Always pay one car off before purchasing your next one.

CHAPTER 8
PASSING OF THE BATON

Preparing the next generation for prosperity

U pon the death of your parents, the leadership of the family passes to you. It will be up to you to carry on the family traditions and take responsibility for the family wealth. That transition is often far from easy.

After all, you have your own lives, interests, and pursuits. Yet each of you understandably believes that he or she has a stake in what your parents or grandparents bequeathed to the family. Parents often wonder how that can be done fairly though. What if, for example, one child dedicated herself to active involvement in the business while her siblings had little or nothing to do with it?

Let's look at this from your parents' point of view and imagine what they may have been thinking and what concerns you need to make certain you are addressing with each other. These are the thoughts, questions, and concerns I address with parents, and you should see it from their viewpoint.

After all, it's not that the other siblings necessarily avoided hard work, but they may have focused their talents elsewhere than the family business. They may even have moved across the continent or the ocean. Does it make sense for them to gain as much control over the business as the one who rose through the ranks, learned the ropes from Mom or Dad, and came to understand the business intimately? However, if they do not get a portion of the business, how will they get a portion of the wealth? Often, there are no easy solutions, and parents just make the best decisions they can.

As you can imagine, a family's assets can break down in a multitude of ways. Sometimes it's not about a business but a different type of asset. What if a child even inherits a stake in a property that does not produce income or that actually comes at a cost? If they lack the resources to cover their part of those costs, they are actually being saddled with quite a burden. I often see this when children inherit a vacation property that they all love but all of them don't have the resources to pay a share of the expenses.

Such complications highlight the importance of careful planning on the front end, working out what is important to the family as a whole and what is important to each individual. The reality is your parents probably did what they thought was the best. It is sometimes in the best interest of the children that they receive different types of assets, depending upon their situations and inclinations.

For example, let's say that there are three children in a family. One has long been devoted to the family business. Another has long been enamored with the family's vacation property at the shore. And the third child has outside interests and may even be working internationally. If the children thought about it logically rather than emotionally, they would all agree that the scenario calls for an *equitable*, rather than an *equal*, distribution of assets among them. Nonetheless, there is plenty of potential for hurt feelings if those discussions don't happen in advance, and advanced planning will go a long way toward avoiding arguments that can split families apart. In fact, heirs can be involved in the decision making. However, that is probably not a good idea when dealing with juveniles or even with immature adults in their twenties. But when leaving resources to "children" who are in their fifties, the situation might call for their active participation. Their perspectives could be valuable. Those children in their fifties or older also need to be responsible enough to initiate the conversations even if their parents haven't.

Hopefully, parents will be reading this section as well as their children and will start as early as possible. It is always wise to thoroughly grasp what is important to those who will be receiving the assets, which means that both the children and the parents need to have conversations about these topics. Once that is thoroughly understood, it is time to talk about the various strategies for making it happen. Those strategies can range from simple to complex. There may be a need to create additional liquidity to provide cash assets for a child who does not want to become a partner in the business. Or the strategy may be to sell the company to someone within the family, allowing that person to take control and move it forward while providing the parents with retirement assets. The best approach will depend upon the family situation and the desired results. Since this topic could be a book in and of itself, I have decided to include a list of techniques in the appendix as a place to start your education on specific estate-planning concepts rather than go into all of the various scenarios. That way you can quickly find items that appeal to you and reach out to your team for additional information on how, or if, it applies to your situation.

Regardless of the goals, one of the keys is to have open communication. It can work wonders in helping these strategies flow smoothly. Often by just talking things through, a family can clear up any misunderstandings and either confirm they are on the right track or prevent a potential mistake in the future. Just because the parents feel the solution was equal or equitable does not mean that the children will feel the same way, especially if they are in the dark as to the reasoning. The more you talk about it, the more everyone will feel they had their say. The feedback is important. An inheritance should catch no one by surprise. No one should be begrudging anyone else the relative size of the bequests. However, when push comes to shove, sometimes the parents have to make a decision that isn't popular with one or more of the children. No parent wants to be in these difficult situations, but it is up to them to decide if they want the family to have a chance to mend any hurt feelings while they are still alive and help or prefer to leave a bomb to go off when the family is already hurting from their loss.

A common situation that is resolved by doing advance planning and involving the heirs is the recognition that there may be a liquidity issue when it comes time to pay taxes. Children who cannot afford the taxes can feel trapped by the inheritance. Sometimes the only way to provide the required liquidity is to sell the property or business, but if the conversation happens in advance, planning can take place to begin transferring the assets earlier or even something as simple as having the liquidity come from the payment of a life insurance benefit.

Even if the family has enough liquidity to pay the taxes and leave the business intact, that doesn't necessarily solve the issue. Let's say that a family has a highly successful business that is by far its largest asset. The parents have three children, one of whom now runs the company and wants to continue doing so, and the other two have no interest and may even be disruptive. The parents nonetheless believe that the business should be divided equally into thirds. After all, they figure, they have paid a good salary to the son who has been running it, so why should he get a bigger piece of the pie? Upon inheriting the company, the two uninvolved siblings have no interest and want to sell it to their brother. He doesn't want them as partners and decides to go deeply into debt to buy them out, but then the economy falters, business slows, and he struggles to make those debt payments, to the point where the normal slow point in the business cycle and heavy debt become too much and the business starts to fail. Eventually he can't afford to keep up the arrangement, because the cash flow just won't work.

The parents had just wanted to treat their children fairly. They wanted to see all of their children do well, with no favoritism. The consequence, however, is the loss of the business that they nurtured and grew for so many years. It was their pride, and a rock of the community, and now it is gone or in the hands of strangers.

One solution is to provide the required liquidity. Life insurance is often used in such situations, so that at the time of the transition, there will be enough cash for one child to buy out the others. That way, the parents who founded the business can feel reassured that they have treated each of their children fairly, and they took an important step to ensure that the family enterprise remains in the bloodline. A common complaint about insurance is the expense; however, no one considers the cost of the alternative: having a child who is burdened with debt trying to pay off their siblings and having to make both interest and capital payments, all while the business transitions ownership. In those terms, the insurance is often cheap, especially if it was held outside of the estate and is not subject to the estate tax.

Alternatively, sometimes the parents will decide to leave a controlling interest in the business to one child and a nonvoting minority interest to the others. The nonvoting minority interest receives cash flow from the business but otherwise has no power or influence on it. On the face of it, this seems like a great idea, but what I have seen in such cases is that the arrangement might start out just fine, but the child who is in charge eventually feels upset that they are doing all the work while the siblings simply receive the payouts. They come to see their sibling as freeloaders or armchair quarterbacks.

At the same time, the siblings with the minority interest sometimes will feel that the parents chose the wrong person to run the business, but at this point they can't do anything about it. In truth, the parents might very well have made the wrong choice. Perhaps the child running the business is not the sharpest of the siblings, but that child got the position because he or she was available and had not shown an inclination to venture out into the world to pursue other interests. Whether the siblings are right or wrong about the situation, the hard feelings fester.

Business owners need to take a hard look at how they are arranging the transition. They need to carefully consider in advance whether they are choosing the right child to run the enterprise or if the child even wants to be responsible for the company without the parent there to work with them. They need to think about issues—not just money but also control. They may decide that it would be best to sell it to an independent party outside the family. That could be far better than setting up divisive forces within the family. Whatever the decision, the earlier these matters can be settled, the less likely it is that deep and divisive issues will develop.

Once again, relationships are at the root of both the potential problems and the potential solutions. When the business owner is considering all the angles for transitioning to the next generation, the loving thing to do is to make sure that the arrangement is set up in a way that does not pit sibling against sibling. Family harmony needs to be preserved. The integrity of the family should always come first.

The reasons why I have included this information in this section of the book is because I think it is important for the inheriting generations to understand that the founders of a family fortune never intend for their assets to be divisive. They want to create an enduring legacy, and the best way to do that is to identify the ultimate goal in advance and design the strategy for getting there smoothly and involve as many of the applicable parties

> "Once again, relationships are at the root of both the potential problems and the potential solutions."

as possible. Again, this calls for open communication and professional guidance, and often it is not the parents who are unwilling or lack the maturity to have the discussion but you the inheritors. The solution might be relatively simple, but you cannot get there until you identify and discuss the problem.

When this process is done correctly, the family business can survive for another generation. Unfortunately, it is seldom done right. The odds are not good that a family business will stand the test of time. Why? Without proper planning, it may be the weakest, not the strongest, family member chosen as successor. Or the best person is selected but she was never mentored on how to operate the business. Either way, the family squabbling often becomes so fierce that nothing gets accomplished, or the company goes so deeply into debt trying to buy out the other parties that it takes on excessive risk and eventually fails.

Thoughtful and thorough planning can avoid all of that. The key is to identify what is needed, whether it is additional liquidity or a well-designed executive structure to which everyone agrees from the start. Once those decisions are made, successful families will start training the successors as early as possible. There should be no surprises. The planning should proceed with openness and clear expectations. Everyone should understand why the family is taking these steps and how it all works.

A FAMILY INVESTED IN ITSELF

A concept I see as gaining more and more traction is the "family investment bank," in which a formal structure is set up. This is one opportunity families can use to strengthen their legacies. Often the family investment bank is a business or businesses, some of which are held in trust. Members of the family serve as the board and have voting rights to make decisions on the direction of the businesses. As with most boards, the members can rotate off so that others in the family can take on the role—if this is a large enough concern, it is wise to include at least one outside board member.

The family investment bank is also a way to educate the younger generation by allowing them to become junior members. This way, they can observe and learn before attaining voting rights while still expressing their ideas and bringing them before the board for consideration.

The effect of this structure is to draw the family members together so that everyone feels they have a say in the decisions that affect the family's wealth and with a goal of allocating resources on the family's behalf in a very broad sense. Those decisions might even go beyond the scope of a business and include items such as investing in certain equities or to donating to charities. Or the family could vote to pay for a college education or provide seed money, perhaps as a loan, for a member to launch a business or purchase a house.

As with any other bank, the members must go through procedures to tap into the resources. This is not a handout. For example, an entrepreneur would need to submit a business plan, and the family would weigh the risks and advantages before deciding whether to take on the proposal. This is a way that families can benefit financially from working together while demonstrating this value and educating younger members. This allows a family of means to strengthen its bonds and develop the talents of its members through education and investment in their worthy pursuits. Many forces are at work to dissipate a family's wealth; this is a way to fight back.

Starting a family bank that operates in a meaningful way requires approximately $2 million or more. Some families begin at a lower level with a family foundation or a donor-advised fund, which similarly helps to forge those family bonds and develop its charitable inclinations, albeit without the business structure. But the idea is the same: the younger members become involved in financial decision making and feel an increasing stake in what becomes of the family wealth. They learn lessons on asset management and how to judge whether an organization is worthy.

Either way, the goal is to maintain the wealth through the generations, as an increasing number of relatives receive a portion of it. It is essential that the family come together for a meeting of the minds on how this wealth will benefit them collectively. Within a few generations, as the family grows, there may be fifty or one hundred descendants making their way in the world, and these steps will have set a precedent for family unity and growth. That cannot happen simply by passing along money. It must come with knowledge, education, and values. The money must be accompanied by a sense of stewardship. By giving the next generation the opportunity to witness what has worked in the past, and by showing them why and how it has worked, the elders of a family will make strides toward preserving the wealth.

The overarching theme is *family solidarity*. That is why it is so important to think through how to transition assets to the next generation—so that the family remains united and not divided. It starts with knowledge, on the parts of both the elders and the up-and-coming leadership. All decisions must be made in a way that will help the family, not hurt it, and that distinction is not always easily discerned. By seeking out professional guidance and keeping the lines of communication wide open, you will be on the way to an enduring prosperity.

I think of our daughters and of the dreams that Dianne and I have for them. We want them to reach for great things, not only attaining prosperity but making this world a better place. These are the things that any loving parents would want their children to accomplish. I believe that if we impart wisdom and structure as part of the legacy of wealth we create, we would be proud of how it will affect our family tree over future generations. It's all about family. That's where it starts, and that's where it grows.

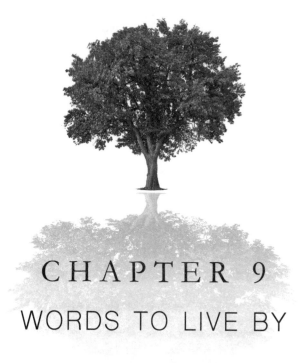

CHAPTER 9
WORDS TO LIVE BY

Parting thoughts for my children

As I think about the importance of transferring wisdom as well as wealth to the next generation, I have given a lot of thought to the values that I would like my family to embrace going forward. Too often, things go unsaid in families. Here, I will say them (or at least some of them). This is what I would want our daughters to know and understand and for them to pass on to their own children if by chance I could not be here to tell them these things in person.

Most of what I have to say in this chapter will not be directly related to money, and that is because unless you have the foundation to live a good life, money won't much matter, not to mention you will be more likely to squander it. These are what my parting words to my children would be, and I share them with you in the hope that you will find the inspiration to draw closer to your own families.

Fulfillment leads to success, and success leads to wealth— not the other way around. Most people chase success, and when they get it, they find that it is not what they assumed it would be. Success comes naturally to those who do what they love, what they enjoy, what they do well, and what matters most to them. A lot of people try to force their way to success, but they gain no satisfaction from it. The success is short-lived and soon will feel meaningless. Unless you are doing something fulfilling, success won't matter to you, and it won't last.

Focus on the process, not the results. Your goal should be to do something you love and find fulfillment in the process of creating it, like a great artist does. If you love the doing, then you will be consistently fulfilled and content. Life will still throw you curves, and you will have times of unhappiness, but through it all you will feel a sense of satisfaction—and to live a satisfying life is the mark of success. When you simply chase success, you might get momentary feelings of elation at times, but eventually you will think, *Is that all there is?* Your reward should be coming from deeper within you.

When an artist creates a masterpiece, that great work simply reflects the artist's mastery of the process. We enjoy the end result, but what motivated the artist was the love of doing it.

It's all in the journey. It's what we do along the way that matters. If you are not enjoying the journey, you probably are not doing the right thing. Your success will feel forced. I am not at all saying that success is unimportant. We should try to succeed in life. What I am saying is that success is the standard by which you judge the process. You still might need to tweak that process to get the desired results, and you will want to work consistently toward improving yourself and the processes to attain the best outcomes. We can always get better. And if you are feeling a sense of satisfaction, you will know you are on the right track. And you will not be trying to fill a void, which can lead to bad habits. Rather, you will feel as if you are building upon a blessing.

Plan your life. A lot of people spend more time planning for a vacation than actually taking it. In my experience, I've found that people actually get more joy from dreaming of the trip than they get from the trip itself. This is because much of the joy lies in the anticipation. They find satisfaction in the process, which can be even better than the end results.

But remember life is a trip, and as with any trip, plans change and you will need to make course corrections to get to where you need to be. Those adjustments in life will help you save time, money, and effort. You will recognize opportunities as they become available to you. You will feel inclined to use your gains in life to lift you to further heights and to invest for a brighter future, building on your internal sense of fulfillment rather than spending your time aimlessly in search of external fulfillment that simply doesn't exist. In other words, it is the planning that is important, not the plan; some of those things that take you off your plan will end up being your greatest joys.

> **"In other words, it is the planning that is important, not the plan; some of those things that take you off your plan will end up being your greatest joys."**

Follow the Golden Rule. This is one of life's truisms. We need to treat others as we ourselves would wish to be treated. It works in relationships, and it works in business. Your name is your currency. You cannot control what anybody else thinks, but you can control your own actions. You have the power to do right and to be the person that you believe you should be.

Accept people for who they are, and do not expect that everyone else will meet your standards of behavior. That will only frustrate you. Just come alongside people where they are and accept who they are, showing them by example how you believe others should be treated. For all you know, you are not meeting their expectations. They may have a different perspective, and sometimes it doesn't hurt to take a walk in their shoes. But no matter what, stay who you are, and allow others to be who they are.

Do not expect them to be you, and don't tolerate people who either don't like you for being you or want you to change to the image of what they think you should be.

Practice anonymous acts of kindness. To serve others without expectation of recognition is, I believe, the mark of true charity. If you find yourself upset that someone didn't say "thank you," then perhaps what you did was more for your own benefit than anyone else's. Good deeds that require you be recognized may be more about putting yourself on display than about reaching out to help others. There is nothing wrong with getting recognition, but if that is the sole motivation for your act of kindness, you can hardly call it charity.

I believe children should be encouraged to give anonymously of their own resources. Perhaps they could buy a gift or make a donation during the holidays. They will be giving joy to another child who will not know whom to thank—and that's the point. Parents should explain to their children that anonymous giving is the purest charity.

Be generous with your gratitude. Don't forget how you feel when someone thanks you for a good deed. When others are kind to you, be generous with your gratitude, and think the best of them.

Be a giver, not a taker—life is too short. Some people, when they walk into a room, make you smile. When others walk in, you just know that they are there to ask you for something. Do your best to be the one who brings a smile to other people's faces. Be the one who will reach out a hand to help, not to get a handout.

Try to be the sort of person who builds other people up and energizes them, not one who drains them. Embrace people who are of a like mind in this area. When people with a giving spirit band together, great things happen—both those in the group and the world at large benefit.

Surround yourself with happy people, because when you do, it will be easier to be happy yourself. It is hard not to smile back at someone who is smiling at you. It is equally hard not to scowl back at someone who is scowling at you.

When you choose your friends wisely and associate with those who are giving and happy, you will find yourself becoming more like them in attitude and deed. Be a good friend, and be willing to share your life. Occasionally even those who are takers will see something in your spirit that they want to emulate, or they will become frustrated that they can't bring you down to their level and move on.

Do not do anything you would not tell your kids or your grandparents. If you would not want them to know what you are up to, then perhaps you shouldn't be up to it. Some matters are private, of course, and I'm not saying you have to live your life by someone else's standards. But if you are acting secretive and feel as though you are living a double life, something is clearly wrong. If you would be ashamed to tell your loved ones about something you have done, then do not do it. Do not post anything online that you would not want your kids or grandparents to see, and do not go anywhere online where you would not want them to go. That's good advice whether you're dealing with matters of morality or matters of money. Do not put your money in places where you would not advise your kids or your grandparents to put it either.

Say yes to life and no to danger. Try new things, even if they feel scary. Too often, people shut themselves off and say no to everything. You need to take some calculated risks if you are to prosper and feel a sense of adventure. Try some things that you might not know you would be interested in. Spend some time outside your comfort zone. Life is both more interesting and fun that way.

Certainly there are times to say no, such as to activities that are immoral or dangerous to you, either physically, spiritually, or to your reputation. Sometimes, people will try to take advantage of you, so follow your moral compass. Consider again the litmus test of whether this is something about which you would tell your kids or your grandparents.

The ability to distinguish between when to say yes and no comes from experience, from living and learning, and from taking the good counsel of people you trust. Always stay true to yourself. Some people will try to lead you astray, and naysayers will try to talk you out of the mission that you have set for yourself. They will not understand your passion. But if you truly believe in what you are doing, then stay the course. If you are going to make a change, you should be excited about it.

Have a variety of friends. Variety is the spice of life. Reach out to other communities and other ideas. Challenge your beliefs, and challenge theirs. In my opinion, the world has stopped having a dialogue and instead is having a diatribe—be bigger and broader than that.

Some thoughts on marriage. Read *The Gift of the Magi* by O. Henry. It is a beautiful tale about sacrificial giving. Marry a giver who cares about your happiness and whose smile makes you smile. The best relationships are the ones in which each person gets joy from making the other happy. As corny as it sounds, I'm happy when I feel that I've made Dianne happy. She feels happy when she makes me happy. Satisfaction builds upon satisfaction. Giving leads to more giving, and the joy grows. That cannot happen if you marry a taker instead of a giver. You will feel dissipated instead of motivated.

Be very careful about whom you choose for your lifelong mate. It is among life's biggest decisions, and both you and your spouse need to be willing to work on the relationship. Marry someone who makes you want to be a better person. Do not marry someone who wants to change you but rather someone who inspires you to want to change.

Do not borrow trouble. In other words, do not spend your life worrying about what might be. Most of the things that we worry about in life never actually happen. Yes, it is important to plan for your future, to save and invest and protect yourself from future trouble. It is important to prepare, but that does not mean you should be worrying all the time. If you feel secure about the future, you can live more in the moment. Don't waste your time fretting about troubles that may never come.

Listen more than you talk. People will appreciate you more. You will learn more. You're a better friend if you listen more than you talk, and you can learn a lot by listening when it comes to financial matters. Hear how people are dealing with money in their homes, marriages, and workplaces. Then think about how what they have said might apply to your own situation, both positively and negatively.

It's tough to learn when your mouth is moving. I know this is true in my role as a financial advisor, and I know that it is true in my roles as father, husband, and friend. You cannot get to the bottom of matters when you are doing most of the talking. You need to hear people out, with an attitude of respect. I listen closely to my young daughters because they have problems and issues that are worlds apart from mine. How could I hope to understand unless I've listened intently to what they are telling me?

Have diverse friendships. Yes, this is the second time I have mentioned this, which tells you how important it is for you to grow as a person. This will make you a better and more interesting person. Become close to people of different ethnicities, cultures, financial statuses, ages, and political leanings. Think of it this way: if all of your friends were in the same room and they were completely comfortable with one another, then you probably do not have a diverse enough group of friends. You will benefit greatly by expanding your circle to include a variety of interesting perspectives, and frankly, you will have more fun! You will also grow to be more tolerant because it is much more difficult to discriminate against a friend or an idea that comes from a friend. If your friends only reflect yourself, you will not learn nearly as much.

Do not judge. Always put yourself in the other person's shoes. Consider what others have been through and what they are going through. You cannot possibly know all the reasons why people behave or act as they do, and so you can't be the judge. There is only one true judge, and that is not you. Abide by your own standards, but if you feel that someone else is falling short of them, remember the old saying: "There, but for the grace of God, go I." When you feel frustrated, whether with your job or with other things that life sends your way, pause to consider that things could be worse. Appreciate what you have, even as you strive for better.

Be respectful of those who provide you a service. If they're performing a job that you would not want to do yourself, thank them. What they are doing is honorable. You may be better off than they are financially, but they deserve your courtesy and respect. If they are doing the best they can and taking pride in their work, you should give them respect—whether they are a surgeon or a ditch digger. In fact, such people are even more deserving of your respect than those who make considerably more money but feel no pride and put forth minimal effort. There is honor in a job well done.

The flip side of that is when it may be one of those times in your life where you may not be in your ideal job, do the best you can while you are there. Learn what you can. Look for lessons that will serve you well in your future endeavors, and consider it an investment in yourself. That's the best investment you can make because it is only when you are investing in yourself that others will want to invest in you. To this day, I feel one of my most formative work experiences was when I waited tables for a short period of time in college. I learned more about humanity and hard work while waiting tables than at any other point in my professional life.

No matter how bad you think things are, you can always start again. Life goes on. The tragedies of today, even the traumatic ones, tend to fade from memory as time goes by. Sometimes you even end up laughing about them. Sometimes you see that a difficulty that you faced with a loved one served to bind you together.

In any case, you can always start from scratch. You can always pursue a new opportunity, perhaps in a new community. You can look for greater possibilities. Every day is a new beginning; you never have to think of it as the end. Never give up. If need be, just start anew. Make the most of the time that is yours, and do

"There are always second chances in life."

not give it over to despair. There are always second chances in life.

Spend time in meditation. Or at least take a couple minutes every day to yourself for some introspective thinking. It will make you a better person. When you take the time to reflect upon your day or your direction in life, you will gain perspective and peace of mind—and it might even end up as a nap!

SECTION THREE REVIEW

I started this book while on summer vacation with the family and am finishing my first draft on Thanksgiving weekend, as Dianne is decorating the house for Christmas. She is rushing because she wants it to be done before we pick up the girls from their grandparents' house. It is our holiday tradition that they come home from their grandparents' to a decorated house.

This entire book has revolved around family, and almost all of my writing has been done with the sounds of family around me. Whether it was a holiday or a soccer practice, family has almost always been in sight. I hope you share this last section as a family and that it brings peace and value to you and your family.

Let's take a look at some of the principles from this section.

Chapter 7

- Here are some things that parents should communicate to their children to prepare them to be good stewards:
  - Talk to them about the meaning of money. Make sure they understand the value of a dollar. Even if you have extensive resources, do not hesitate to say no to them when they ask for something that has no value.
  - Explain credit, both the good uses and the bad uses.
    - o good: long-term assets that increase in value
    - o bad: anything that depreciates or will be completely consumed before you pay off the bill
  - Explain to them that an attitude of gratitude will lead to happiness, but an attitude of entitlement will lead to frustration and failure.

- They should have a part-time job at some point in order to understand the value of money, as well as to pay for things they think they want.
- Explain that whatever they receive from you, now or in the future, is a gift and is not an entitlement. Tell them that if you feel they will not be good stewards of those gifts, they will not receive them.
- Explain the value of compounding money and that financial success is a marathon, not a sprint.

Chapter 8

- When deciding how to divide resources among the next generation, you want to be fair and equitable—that does not mean the same thing as *equal*. *Equal* is not always *fair*.
- Update your estate plan:
  - basic will
  - powers of attorney (different types)
  - trusts, when needed for your family's protection
- Review Estates A–Z in the appendix.
- Involve the children when appropriate, especially if they will have responsibilities.
- If appropriate, start discussing gifting strategies.
- Start your family investment bank while you are alive. Discuss with your family what can be included and how it will affect them in the long term.

Chapter 9

- Here is a short list of words to live by:
  - ◻ Be thankful. No one owes you anything, and you are entitled to nothing, so be grateful for everything.
  - ◻ Follow the Golden Rule—with everyone, not just your peers.
  - ◻ Do not judge.
  - ◻ Always work to improve yourself. If you do not invest in you, who else will?
  - ◻ Take risks, and go on adventures. If you are bored, it's your own fault. Life is meant to be lived. If you are not scared occasionally, you may be missing out on some of the best things in life.
  - ◻ Fail! If you never fail, how will you know whether you have reached your potential? How will you know what you need to improve? You can achieve more than you could ever imagine—you just have to try.
  - ◻ Your character is what you do when no one is looking. If you would not tell your grandparents or children about it, then do not do it, say it, or post it.
  - ◻ Ignore peer pressure. Do not listen to those who try to pressure you into something you do not want to do. They are either scared or they want to drag you down with them. If you fall to their pressure, you will be letting yourself down, and you will be enabling them.

CONCLUSION
NO TIME LIKE THE PRESENT

Much of this book has been a journey through time. We have examined the concerns and challenges at each stage in a lifetime. These pages have included advice for young people beginning a career, for couples, and for those who have lost a spouse. I have shared concepts here that are important to people just starting out and to those contemplating the best way to pass on their legacy. Life comes in seasons, with different priorities in each—but when it comes to planning for the future, there is no time like the present.

It is easy to say that you will take care of things tomorrow, but what if your tomorrow never comes? Have you considered that? I know that I have. I want my family to be prepared. That is why I have written this book. Much of what you have read is what I wish my own family to understand. I have addressed it to a broader audience because I know I am not alone in wanting the best for my loved ones. I want them to move forward with confidence, guided by the voice of a father and husband who cared to share with them these observations and meditations, even if he couldn't be there in person.

Each of us today is living the legacy we will leave behind. We are creating something that we can be proud of, something that will extend beyond us. We must make the right decisions now and in the future if that legacy is to thrive. Finances, of course, are a part of it but not all of it. This has not been a book on how to manage your money. My purpose was to write a book about how to manage your wealth—and wealth is about far more than money. You are investing in the prosperity of your entire family tree, and much of that is a matter of the heart.

It all starts with the family, with caring and communication. Family leaders need to share their dreams and rally their loved ones to accomplish more than they might have imagined. That is how you attain true wealth and a legacy that lives for generations.

This section of the book follows a different format and is a review of some basic estate-planning information. You can either read it as a part of the book or utilize it as a reference guide.

APPENDIX 1: ESTATE-PLANNING BASICS AND COMMON JARGON

THE WHAT AND THE WHO

One of the first questions you may be asking yourself is should I, or more accurately when should I, do estate planning? The reality is that you need to do it now, whether you are twenty or ninety, rich or poor. If you have anything to give or leave and you want to have some say as to how that happens, you need to do some planning or at the very least confirm that the laws of the state you live in will accomplish what you want. Because, in the simplest terms, if you don't create a plan of your own you are choosing to use the plan of the state you live in. (Each state has its own default plan.) And most people I know don't want the state to make every decision for how their cherished assets will be distributed, so let's get to work and get this taken care of.

Now before I write another word, I need to say—both because I legally need to say it and because I truly believe it—see a lawyer and a CPA! I am not giving legal or tax advice in this section I am telling you the generalities you need to have a good conversation with an estate attorney or CPA. The rules change every day and on a state-by-state basis—it is very important to make sure you get the right counsel with your estate plan. I have no issues with people who want to do financial things themselves (although I obviously believe professional advice adds value), but in this case I am telling you not to do it yourself. Seek counsel! By definition, because you have to die to put your estate plan in action, if you make a mistake you will not be around to correct it and will just be leaving a mess for your family. This is the hardest part of the financial-planning process for many people and the one they are most afraid of doing wrong. The good news is that does not have to be the case. As you have heard me say more than once—start off by just taking a deep breath and relaxing. There is no right or wrong way to do an estate plan (as long as you stay within the confines of the law—which are broad in most cases). And unless you elect to do something that is irrevocable (more on this later) you can always make changes. For that matter, not only can you but you probably will need to make changes every couple of years. As both your life and wealth changes and the lives and wealth of those that will benefit from your plan changes you want to update your plan along the way. An easy example of this is planning for children. What you do to protect them when they are two years old will probably be significantly different than what you will need to do when they are fifty-two years old.

In the broadest terms, having an estate plan is really just you directing the disposition of your assets both during your life and after your death. What you may not have realized is that every time you open an account or purchase an asset, you are acting on your estate plan either consciously or unconsciously. For example, when you opened your 401(k) plan at work, did you list a beneficiary? That was estate planning. When you bought your house, did you do it jointly? Another piece to your estate plan. How about that new bank account—is it individual, joint, or maybe even payable on death (POD)? That was estate planning. In other words, you have already made hundreds of small estate-planning decisions over your lifetime. Creating the formal plan is really just putting all of those pieces together and deciding if that is what you intended or if you need to make changes.

An analogy that comes to mind is that it is a little like decorating your house. Sometimes you can take the same items and rearrange them and everything works perfectly (changing beneficiaries), sometimes you find out you have more than you need and you want to simplify things (sell assets or donate to charity), sometimes you realize you may want to add some special item or protect a family heirloom (possibly set up a trust or buy insurance). Another time you may realize that the house you live in no longer fits your needs and it is time to move (create a whole new estate plan). Either way, making conscious decisions improves the outcome and, for most getting professional help (your financial team and especially your estate planner), goes a long way to getting the outcome you are looking for.

Having said all of that, there is an order of importance to what you need to accomplish. Although your order may be different than mine, or you might be at a different stage of life, there are some basics that you will need to cover.

I recommend starting with your immediate family and its immediate needs. The simplest place to start is setting up the proper documents for who makes the decisions when you can't any longer either because you are deceased or incapacitated.

Following are some sample questions you will need to prepare for:

- Who takes care of your minor children (assuming you have any)?
- Who takes care of your financial matters and makes financial decisions on your behalf? This can range from

paying bills while you are incapacitated to investing for future generations.

- Who makes your health-care decisions?
- Who will be your executor (the person that manages your estate at your passing)?
- And if you are single (or would prefer that your spouse not make these decisions), who can make decisions about your funeral? With the ever-increasing percentage of alternative family arrangements, we are seeing problems in this area more and more frequently.

After you have answered those basic questions, you then start to tackle the more complex questions, which involve perpetuating your family values and tax planning. Take note that I put tax planning last because if you don't do the first ones correctly there are worse things that can happen than the government getting a larger share of your estate than the absolute minimum.

COMMON TOOLS AND TERMS OF ESTATE PLANNING

LAST WILL AND TESTAMENT

These are the basic directions for probate. (I will cover probate in just a minute, but I have to start somewhere, and most people have heard about a will.) The big thing to be aware of is that a will can be argued, fought, sometimes even ignored (especially if there are parts that ignore the law). Normally the directions given in a will are followed, but that is not always the case, and not every asset you own will necessarily be covered by your will or the probate court.

Remember that this involves the law, and each state has its own rules so please speak to an estate planner who is a lawyer to confirm that it applies to your situation. First let's take a look at what is actually covered in your will and what decisions you have already made and how that affects our will and estate.

OWNERSHIP

One of the first things that are looked at is if there is a joint owner on the account—especially if he or she is listed as joint with rights of survivorship. For example, Dianne and I have our personal family checking account listed this way. So what happens if I get hit by a truck—or what if I fall off of the ladder hanging Christmas lights and impale myself on an animatronic reindeer? The account becomes Dianne's—it doesn't go through probate, no one can really argue with her about it—basically she shows up with a death certificate and possibly another form or two proving I am no longer, and the account is hers to do what she will. No muss, no fuss, and no further control by me. She can do with it as she will. This is true of almost any jointly held assets—sometimes a state will have some rules just to make sure that everything is on the up and up, but in rough terms it is normally that simple.

But what if I own an account individually and it is not owned jointly or in a form of joint ownership that states that the assets are to be divided (an example of this is tenants in common—think of it like having a roommate for an asset)?

CONTRACT BENEFICIARY

We have identified that it is not a jointly owned asset, so what do they do next? They see if there is a contractual agreement in place. The two most common forms of this I see are a beneficiary designation or a trust.

Let's start with the beneficiary designation. In simplest terms when you sign a form with a beneficiary designation you are signing a contract that states that you want whoever is holding those assets to give them to the beneficiary at your passing and to not be included in the probate process (still included in your estate for estate tax purposes though). Anytime you open a qualified retirement account or almost any form of insurance that has a death benefit you are going to be asked who the beneficiary is. Additionally, sometimes when you open a standard brokerage account or bank account you normally also have the option of making it payable on death (POD) or transferable on death (TOD). Similar to what happens if you own an asset jointly, a listed beneficiary normally supersedes directions given in the will, meaning those assets go to whoever is listed as beneficiary. This makes tracking and changing your beneficiaries extremely important, especially if there is a life change such as a divorce or death. For example, it is extremely common for someone to never update their beneficiary designation after a divorce and then have retirement account or life insurance proceeds go to an ex-spouse instead of their children or their new spouse. Sometimes—and only sometimes—this can be fixed, but even in those circumstances it is a painful process for everyone involved.

The other common way we see something transfer by contract is if there is a trust involved. There are multiple types of trusts, and for the purposes of this part of the conversation the only thing that really matters is that almost all of them name a beneficiary (even if it is just the estate). The easiest way to think of this is that you are creating an entity (trust) that is normally designed to either live beyond you and continue based upon the rules you set for it or an entity that will disperse the assets in a specific way (many times into another trust) before they get to probate.

PROBATE

If you have read the previous sections, you may already realize that probate just takes into account what is left over (isn't jointly owned, in a trust, or have a beneficiary designation), what the law says must be probated (varies by state), or potentially what the inheritors are fighting over and feel they have a better chance in probate court.

It is better to think of probate as a process rather than just a specific thing. The four major parts of the process are:

1. File a petition with the probate court, and give notice to interested parties. Part of the filing of the petition involves admitting the will to the court and selecting an executor or, if there isn't a will, the court normally appoints an administrator. This also gives interested parties an opportunity to begin to argue the selection of the executor or court-appointed administrator.

2. The executor or administrator has to notify the deceased creditors so they can make a claim against the estate and also create an inventory (and normally a value) for all the assets that will be included in the probate process (quick reminder—this is different than the total assets for tax purposes because it does not include assets that were jointly owned and passed to the joint owner or assets that

have beneficiaries—to put it bluntly, your total estate that the IRS looks at is normally bigger than the portion of the estate that will be probated).

3. Taxes, debts, funeral expenses are paid out of the estate. This follows a waiting period that is different on a state-by-state basis and normally a process to verify the validity of the debts. Once verified, accounts may be liquidated or assets sold to accomplish the paying off all of these various expenses.

4. Once the waiting period is over, the personal representative or executor then petitions the court to distribute the assets as prescribed by the will (subject to the applicable laws) or if there was no will by the state's probate law. Conflict can easily arise here based on the distribution of assets—which is one of the reasons this is done by petitioning the court's approval before ownership is changed. (Quick reminder—this is done after the taxes and other debts are paid, so what is eventually disbursed is really what is left over from the estate.)

TRUSTS

This topic is a book in and of itself—however, let's keep it simple. A trust is an artificially created entity (legal construct) that holds assets for the benefit of someone (a beneficiary) other than the trust itself.

For most trusts, the most important thing to know is what type of trust it is and the identity of the three roles that are normally part of the trust agreement. The first role is the trust itself. It normally consists of the trust agreement (the rules the trust operates under), which gives directions as to how the trust is supposed to operate and the trust assets to be managed. The second role is the trustee—this is the person or entity who follows the rules set forth in the trust agreement. Finally we have the beneficiary (in a limited number of circumstances, this is the same person as the trustee), which is the person who is supposed to receive benefits from the trusts (this can be more than one person or even more than one generation of people).

As for types, there are many subsets that fall under two broad categories: revocable and irrevocable. The easiest is the *revocable* trust— just like the name suggests, you can change it at will. I normally see these trusts utilized to avoid probate or in preparation for a day when a person may no longer be able to act for his or her own benefit. There is seldom any tax benefit from a revocable trust.

The second category is *irrevocable*—as the name suggests, once it is completed and funded, it is very difficult to pull the assets back out or change the terms. However, over time many state legislatures have become more flexible and allow irrevocable trusts to be modified within a range of time by the beneficiaries if they go to court. It should go without saying and is true of this entire portion of the book, but seek legal advice in your state because many of the operating laws are on a state-by-state basis. The primary reason I see irrevocable trusts is to try to control assets from the grave, creditor and predator protection for the beneficiaries, and to help with estate tax issues. Often, irrevocable trusts are set up during a person's life to gift assets into; other times, they are not funded until death.

FUNERAL DIRECTIVES

Funeral directives are something I never used to see but are becoming more frequently added to estate-planning documents and may be worth considering depending on your situation. The basic idea is that if you want someone other than your closest *legal* family member to make decisions about your funeral you have to give him or her the authority to do it.

A couple of common situations where this applies is unmarried couples—because there is *no* legal agreement between them, the surviving partner has no legal standing to make decisions as to the disposition of the body. If there is ill will between the surviving partner and the deceased family, they may run the risk of being totally shut out of the process.

This potentially could happen if your closest relative has different religious views, they may try to impose their wishes rather than yours. Or it could even be left to an estranged spouse where a divorce decree was never finalized.

In simplest terms if you want someone other than your closest legal family member to make the decisions, you need to set up the proper funeral directives for this to happen.

LIVING DOCUMENTS

Along with your estate-planning documents, there are three additional documents that are commonly misunderstood and should be done with your estate plan but aren't really a part of it.

The reason I say this is because the moment you die, all three of them become useless. They help until that point but stop when you do.

1. **Power of Attorney (POA)**

There are multiple varieties with different levels of power, but in the simplest terms any POA gives someone the ability to act on your behalf. These powers can be broad and always available, as is the case with many durable

POAs, or they can be limited either in the scope of what they allow—such as a trading authorization—or possibly only be used when certain events happen such as someone being mentally unable to act on their own behalf (springing powers).

Two areas of caution: only give someone your POA if you really trust them because you are giving them control, and also remember that when you die those powers stop immediately. This is a big point of confusion for many people. At your death, the POA stops and the executor steps in—no more action can be taken on the directions of a POA after someone is deceased.

2. **Health-Care Directives**

These are similar to funeral directives but for while you are still living and unable to make decisions on your own behalf. This covers most of the big end-of-life decisions and allows you to leave directions or appoint the person you would like to make the decisions on your behalf. As a quick note, if you are asking someone else to make these decisions on your behalf, realize that you are generally passing on a large burden especially if you have parties that will not be in agreement. This is similar to selecting an executor, which is both an honor and a burden—read the poem I listed in that section. It is a little tongue in cheek but not far off at all.

3. HIPAA

This is one of the areas of unintended consequences that we have to deal with in today's world. Because everyone wants their medical information private, doctors and hospitals can no longer share the information without a form being signed that follows HIPAA requirements. Make sure this is taken care of and up to date with current law so your family can get your medical information when they need it.

APPENDIX 2: THE ESTATE- PLANNING TEAM

FINANCIAL PLANNER

A word of caution: anyone can say they are a financial planner or a financial advisor—don't be fooled. Unfortunately this is an area where you need to do a little research and vetting. The easiest first step is to see if they are a CFP®. If they have that designation, they have at least gone through a fairly rigorous curriculum and become board certified. There are a bunch of other certifications (I personally have several), and they can vary from being very difficult to get to extraordinarily easy, so don't get fooled by a bunch of initials. If people hold themselves out as financial planners or financial advisors and they are not CFPs®, ask them why they are not. Ask them how they are qualified to make the recommendations they are making. They may have a valid reason such as a member of their team is a CFP® and puts together the actual plan and recommendations, but if that is the case you should know that up front. If they say they have other financial-planning designations that are as good, I would be very careful. As I said, there are some other quality designations, but they are almost all more limited in their materials or are more specialized.

This is a very important role because the financial planner is often the quarterback of the entire financial relationship and in many situations their primary job may be to act as a generalist who brings in specialists to cover a specific issue or to help coordinate among the various specialists as appropriate.

ATTORNEY

Don't draft anything without an attorney! Seek their advice! I won't put an exclamation point after this one, but make sure he or she is an estate attorney. You don't want a litigator, business lawyer, or real-estate lawyer to do your documents. I can't stress this enough—these have to be done correctly; otherwise it can be a nightmare for the family. Remember by definition you won't be able to explain your intentions since you will have passed. A good estate attorney may cost you a little more than a general practitioner, but it may save those you care about untold heartache and money. This is not the place to skimp.

ACCOUNTANT

In the same vein as the attorney, get a good CPA who specializes in the type of tax work you need while you are alive. In many instances, they will have less of a direct affect than some of your other financial professionals in regard to your estate plan, but they frequently provide good guidance on an ongoing basis and many times have information that the rest of the team doesn't. And similar to a good lawyer, I frequently will ask a client to ask their CPA if a specific strategy might benefit them. I have a great CPA who is part of my personal team and recommend you do the same.

TRUST ADVISOR

If you are going to have trusts as part of your estate plan, you need someone qualified to discuss how they work in the real world. Later I will go through some information on trustees so I will not belabor the point here. But whoever is going to be the trustee needs to be aware of the details of the document, and you need to be aware of how those details actually will be acted on by a trustee. The trustee is the person who carries your wishes forward, and knowing how they make judgments and how they will have to act on a trust document is extremely important.

LIFE INSURANCE AGENT

The good and the bad. Have you ever heard the line, "If all you have is a hammer than everything looks like a nail"? Well that has a tendency to be true with life insurance agents. Having said that, for most high-net-worth individuals, life insurance can and does play an important part of their estate plan. I will give you a couple of things to look for and a couple of things to avoid when looking for an insurance agent to help with this part of the plan. First, they should have access to multiple carriers (insurance companies), and as a general rule I try to avoid agents who directly work for a single carrier because of the risk of a conflict of interest even if the carrier allows them access to multiple carriers. One of the easiest ways to know if your insurance agent is in that situation is if their company card carries the brand of an insurance company. Additionally, they should work with a broader team of advisors including someone who is a CFP® and a lawyer because good implementation normally requires planning and legal documentation.

This is a bit technical, but one thing I always ask for is the internal rate of return (IRR) for a proposed policy on a *guaranteed*[6] basis—I would consider it a very large red flag if they don't readily provide it or try and show you the *nonguaranteed* IRR.

---

6 All guarantees are subject to the claims paying ability of the issuing insurance company.

APPENDIX 3: TRUST USES

Basic information on what a trust is was covered earlier, but let's take a moment to delve into why we use trusts. As I stated earlier, whole books can be written on this subject, so I will just hit some of the highlights.

No matter the reason, almost all trusts are set up with some thought about financial planning. A starting question is if the planning is initially for the current generation with the assets (normally the grantor), for future beneficiaries, or for both the current generation and future generations.

It often makes sense for many people either at a certain stage of life or because their wealth is significant to begin to utilize trusts for a variety of reasons.

Here are some of the most common reasons:

- to provide a layer of protection for the assets (Specific types of trusts have this characteristic, but not all trusts do. If you are counting on this, make sure the type of trust you have provides this type of protection.)
- beginning the process of active professional investment management
- bill pay, basic recordkeeping, and making certain that all of the tax documents are found and reported
- potential incapacity whether it is temporary or permanent (A permanent example of this is with people with long-term, debilitating illnesses such as Alzheimer's. In those situations, they are alive but do not have the capacity to manage their affairs, and a trust can be a great solution.)
- continuity for a surviving spouse or family (In those situations, the trust can have springing powers so when the

person is no longer capable of making decisions a trustee can step into the role.)

- probate avoidance, as long as you don't name the estate as the beneficiary
- substance abuse problems because you can limit when (if ever) proceeds from the trust go to the potential abuser and even provide for substance abuse counseling
- beneficiaries with poor money management skills
- protection from predators and creditors (Depending on who you are talking to this can range from a level of asset protection in case of divorce to scam artists trying to take advantage of an unsophisticated trust beneficiary.)

One of the things that surprise most people is the wide degree of distributions that can be set up in the terms of the trust. These can range from full access to a commonly used frame of reference called HEMS, which stands for health, education, maintenance, and support. Often there may even be incentive clauses for certain activities like graduating from college, earning a certain income, or buying a first home. In rough terms, if it is legal, you can create a clause in a trust that will try to replicate or incentivize the activities you want or at least not fund the activities you don't.

One of the best uses for trusts is to provide a framework for a family governance program as I mentioned earlier in the book. This can help to direct investments, educational goals, charitable intentions, and the list goes on.

The final reason, but the one most frequently mentioned, is to move assets out of the estate for estate tax-planning purposes. There are multiple structures that are available, and which one is the right fit will depend on your circumstances.

CHOOSING YOUR TEAM WHEN YOU ARE GONE

Two of the most important people (or firms) you will select are the ones who act as your executor/personal representative for the probate process and who is the trustee of your trusts at your passing. This is both an honor and a burden, so choose carefully.

The following poem by Edgar Guest called "The Executor" is about as eloquent a description as any I have seen, and for the most part you can utilize executor, personal representative, or trustee interchangeably.

It starts with how his friend honored him by making him his executor and ends with:

> *His widow once so calm and meek,*
> *Comes, hot with rage, three times a week,*
> *And rails at me, because I must,*
> *To keep my oath appear unjust.*
> *His children hate the sight of me,*
> *Although their friend I've tried to be,*
> *And every relative declares,*
> *I interfere with his affairs.*
> *Now when I die I'll never ask,*
> *A friend to carry such a task,*
> *I'll spare him all such anguish sore,*
> *And leave a hired executor.*

Edgar A. Guest, *Today and Tomorrow*
(Chicago: Reilly & Lee Company, 1942)

As the poem suggests, you may be honoring them, but you are certainly not doing them a favor by making them your executor or as a trustee for your family—it is more of a curse. Few people who have never been in those roles realize the difficult situation that they are being placed, especially if the estate is complex and extends among a large number of assets or a large family. Having said that, there are good reasons to have an individual trustee and to have a corporate trustee. Let's take a look at some of the advantages and disadvantages of both.

PROS AND CONS OF INDIVIDUAL TRUSTEES

They know you and your family. If you trust them enough to play either of those roles, they know the dynamics of the family or where extra care may need to be taken or where there could be a little extra lenience given. Another reason an individual is sometimes the best choice is when there are complex family assets such as a family business or farm and the trustee and/or the executor has the correct experience and can help to guide the asset to its next stage. This can be extremely important if the goal is to keep those assets as legacy assets to be handed down from generation to generation. Finally, the last big benefit of the individual trustee is normally price. Sometimes they will offer to do it for free or at a very low cost. But this is a double-edged sword because over time they often grow tired of the responsibility—especially if they are trustees for decades. They may take their role seriously in the early years, but if it isn't their main revenue source they often become more and more lax and resentful over time and at some point begin to regret accepting the role.

Think if it in these terms: what if someone offered you a job with no (or very little) pay whose primary role was to dole out money for other people. How long would you be interested, even if you really liked the people you were giving the money too?

Another common disadvantage is the risk that there will be a lack of impartiality (real or perceived). A common example is where a trustee allows one beneficiary to purchase a house but won't allow another. The trustee may or may not have a valid reason, but the perception of the beneficiary who was told no will assume it is favoritism.

Individual trustees may not even know the laws that apply to the trusts and end up either putting themselves at financial risk or run the risk of accidentally breaking the trusts. Unfortunately for the trustee, when they accept the responsibility they may also be accepting more risk and work than they realize.

Often there is also the case where the trustee's life span and the trust's are not the same. The new trustee is the contemporary of the people who set up the trust, not the grandchildren who will eventually benefit from it. In other words, before the trust ends the trustees pass away themselves or become incapacitated in such a way that they can no longer carry out the duties.

Finally, an individual trustee may just not have the correct experience to manage the trusts—this is the flip side of needing an individual trustee to help operate the family business. The individual trustee may have never managed money, created disbursements, filed trust tax returns, or a whole host of other duties that being a trustee requires, which takes us to the benefits of a corporate trustee.

PROS AND CONS OF CORPORATE TRUSTEES

They are normally professionally trained and have both individual experience but also often have institutional resources at their firm when needed. This sounds simple, but if you are leaving significant assets, having someone in charge who has been around the block a couple of times makes sense. I would not want to be the first patient of a heart surgeon—similarly I would not want to trust my legacy to a first-time trustee. This is a significant advantage for corporate trustees, especially if there is any complexity to the situation.

Because they are trained and considered professional, if something goes wrong they are normally held to a higher fiduciary standard, which can give the beneficiaries some potential recourse if something goes wrong. And (assuming you pick a large enough institution) they often have audit procedures and the resources to correct an error or breach of duty. Most individuals (and some small firms) don't have those resources, or even if they did, you may not want the beneficiaries to go after the friend or family member you asked to be trustee as a favor.

There is also a level of impartiality because the trustee is not close to the family, and most trust departments have now instituted committees to make discretionary decisions to ensure that impartiality.

A corporate trustee is also long lived—individual trustees may come and go, but the basic methodology of how the trust is managed on a professional basis will be maintained, which can be important, as we see trusts that are often set to last hundreds of years.

Finally they can offer additional services such as bill pay, generational wealth education, sometimes even help facilitate care if a person becomes incapacitated, disabled, or has an addiction issue.

Of course, there are also disadvantages.

The name on the door will probably change over that time as firms merge and acquire each other.

Staff that you may have met when you went to set up the trust may retire or change positions potentially even leaving the firm altogether.

For the extra work that is done and risk that is taken, the corporate trustee normally costs more than a friend or family member doing it as a favor.

The trust may even be too small for it to be cost effective due to the fact most firms now have a minimum fee.

As I mentioned earlier, although a corporate trustee has experience, they do not normally have the experience required to maintain a family business in perpetuity.

The last one I will mention is the perception of inflexibility by the beneficiaries. I actually consider this both a positive and a negative. Remember a corporate trustee's job is to execute the trust as it is written and not to color outside the lines. Most beneficiaries would prefer a trustee that is willing to bend the rules when asked, but most of the people who set up the trusts (you) want the rules to be followed or you would have never set them up that way in the first place.

A COMPROMISE: CO-TRUSTEES

Sometime the best solution is utilizing co-trustees, which consist of the individual trustee and the corporate trustee. This can provide the benefit of having someone who knows the family situation or be able to advise on the family business (the individual trustee) with someone who knows and can apply all of the rules of the trusts to make sure everything is compliant.

This also gives the individual trustee an easy out if there is a request they know is not in the beneficiary's best interest, but they don't want to say no, because they are having Thanksgiving dinner with that person the following week. The individual trustee can request, in private, that the corporate trustee decline the request and take the heat—which is one of the things you are paying them for. Or on the flip side, you can suggest a little leniency with a discretionary request if the individual trustee has a belief based on his knowledge of the beneficiary.

Whatever you choose, make certain to have language so that the beneficiary can change the trustee, because none of us can see into the future. Having said that, in order to keep the beneficiary from moving it to a trustee who might have undue influence, such as a friend or spouse, I do recommend language stating that any change of a trustee has to be made to a new corporate trustee with at least $1 billion in assets in today's dollars, hopefully large enough that they can't be easily influenced by the beneficiaries.

Trey Smith
Private Financial Advisor
SunTrust Investment Services, Inc.
trey.smith@suntrust.com
(615) 463-9023

DISCLAIMER

SunTrust Bank and its affiliates and the directors, officers, employees, and agents of SunTrust Bank and its affiliates (collectively, "SunTrust") are not permitted to give legal or tax advice. While SunTrust can assist clients in the areas of estate and financial planning, only an attorney can draft legal documents, provide legal services, and give legal advice. Clients of SunTrust should consult with their legal and tax advisors prior to entering into any financial transaction or estate plan. Because it cannot provide legal services or give legal advice, SunTrust's services or advice relating to "estate planning" or "wealth transfer planning" are limited to (i) financial planning, multigenerational wealth planning, investment strategy; (ii) management of trust assets, investment management, and trust administration; and (iii) working with the client's legal and tax advisors in the implementation of an estate plan.

These materials are educational in nature. The implications and risks of a transaction may be different from individual to individual based upon past estate, gift and income tax strategies employed, and each individual's unique financial and familial circumstances and risk tolerance.

Investment and insurance products are not FDIC or any other government agency insured and may lose value.

Securities, insurance (including annuities), and investment advisory products and services are offered by SunTrust Investment Services, Inc., a SEC registered investment adviser and broker-dealer affiliate of SunTrust Banks, Inc., member FINRA, SIPC, and a licensed insurance agency.